D0433544

A BOOK OF
HEROES
OR A SPORTING
HALF-CENTURY

A BOOK OF
HEROES
OR A SPORTING
HALF-CENTURY

SIMON
BARNES

First published in 2010 by

Short Books
3A Exmouth House
Pine Street
EC1R 0JH

10 9 8 7 6 5 4 3 2 1

A CIP catalogue record for this book is available from the British Library.

All images © Getty Images
except:
Anita Lonsbrough, Mark Todd, Dancing Brave and Vibart © Press Association

ISBN 978-1-907595-01-1

Printed in Great Britain by Clays, Suffolk

Cover design: Two Associates

Sportswriters, sports editors –
a bizarre and intense relationship.
This one's for the best of them:
Norman Fox
Tom Clarke
David Chappell
Keith Blackmore
Tim Hallissey

50 SPORTING HEROES

1960s

1. *M.J.K. Smith
2. Anita Lonsbrough
3. Don Thompson
4. Abebe Bikila
5. Bobby Charlton
6. Vibart
7. George Best
8. Garry Sobers
9. Bob Beamon
10. Tommie Smith

1970s

11. Olga Korbut
12. Jan Tomaszewski
13. Johan Cruyff
14. Muhammad Ali
15. Colin Cowdrey
16. Arthur Ashe
17. David Steele
18. Bjorn Borg
19. Mike Brearley
20. Fiji

1980s

21. Ian Botham
22. Shergar
23. Torvill and Dean
24. Malcolm Marshall

25. Martina Navratilova
26. David Gower
27. Dancing Brave
28. Ben Johnson
29. Joe Montana
30. Ayrton Senna

1990s

31. Steffi Graf
32. Eric Cantona
33. Florence Griffith-Joyner
34. Mike Atherton
35. Frankie Dettori
36. Pete Sampras
37. Mark Todd
38. Tim Henman
39. Sanath Jayasuriya
40. Katarina Witt

2000s

41. Steve Redgrave
42. Roger Federer
43. Jonny Wilkinson
44. Andrew Flintoff
45. Shane Warne
46. Fu Mingxia
47. David Beckham
48. Ellen MacArthur
49. Usain Bolt
50. Yelena Isinbayeva

1960s

1.*M.J.K. Smith

M.J.K. SMITH OF WARWICKSHIRE and England was my first hero. To this day I have no real idea why. After all, he was never a great cricketer. The election just fell on him. He was there when a vacuum needed to be filled. It certainly wasn't because I saw him as a superman. Right from the first, I was aware of his fallibility: and his every failure caused me a strange, subtle pain. Perhaps the reason I chose Smith – perhaps the reason anybody chooses anybody as a hero – is to know pain. To understand failure. To know sadness. To come to terms with the world's imperfections.

I used to go to the cricket at Edgbaston with my grandfather, day after day of endless sunlit summers, catching the bus at the top of Vicarage Road, King's Heath with our sandwiches neatly parcelled in my grandfather's leather valise. I was about eight when we started. Of course, all the cricketers we saw on those perfect days – days without the least scintilla of boredom – were heroes of a kind: giants in white clothing with an elevated calling, living the brave life in pursuit of runs and wickets and glory, men to whom self-doubt was a stranger.

Smith was their captain: captain of Warwickshire, going on to become captain of England. That's why he had an asterisk before his name. Perhaps it was the asterisk that caused me to single him out: I felt under an obligation to throw in my lot with a person so obviously selected for me. But Smith was not an imposing figure, nor, it must be said, particularly successful. He wore wire-framed glasses that tried to be invisible but failed. These, combined with an awkward smile, made him different from the sculpted stars of *Tiger* comic.

But he was my hero, all the same. Not because I overrated

him: but because I had chosen him. I didn't try to be like him. I didn't think he was a god. I didn't think he was better than everybody else: I just hoped it would turn out that way. Some mysterious process had made him my representative. As a result of this, his successes were my successes: his failures mine.

The notion of the hero has been debased, especially in sport. The term has come to imply uncritical admiration, even worship. It tends to mean "role model", a hideous term, one that seems to insist that it is a child's duty to be as much like his hero as possible: willingly losing his identity in the profound need to be someone else. This is not a legitimate process: it is a personality disorder. And I don't think it actually happens to anyone without a personality disorder: the lie of the role model is a convention that sport, forever puffed up with pride, has invented to boost its own glory. The truth is that a hero is someone who helps you to understand life: helps you to understand how better to enjoy life, and how better to endure it. That is as true of heroes in sport as it is of heroes in fiction and mythology, and it is why heroes matter throughout our lives. Heroes play a large part in the life of a child, but they continue to matter as we grow up, in ways that constantly change and develop. A grown-up's hero is very different from the heroes of children and adolescents, because we slowly learn that heroes and heroism are far more complex than we had supposed. Take Oedipus, for example. Oedipus is a hero all right. He is the hero of his own myth, and of the plays written about him. Oedipus tells us many difficult and profound things. Oedipus matters. But no one has suggested that Oedipus – given to road rage, lechery, power-mania and self-harm – is a role model. He is a much more complex figure than that: and so, for that matter, was M.J.K. Smith. So are all other heroes, and so are the relationships we have with them: vivid, intense, revealing, often painful – and of course, more or less by definition, one-sided.

Smith was nearly great. There is glory in this: also a whiff of tragedy. He was one hell of a games player. He was the last of the double internationals, if you restrict the definition to major sports and reckon it by the date of the last appearance for England. He played one rugby match for England, against Wales in 1956; he played 50 times for the England cricket team, 25 of them as captain, last appearing in 1972. He was a batsman who rebelled against the classical technique of offside strokeplay and hit the ball the other way, to leg, to what he called "the man's side". He would fetch the ball from outside off-stump with pulls and sweeps: a technique that became a new orthodoxy as the game changed. Smith was both a throwback, then, and a man ahead of his time. He was good, too: in 1959, he scored 3,249 runs in the first-class cricket season, unthinkable now. He made more than 2,000 runs in six consecutive seasons. He liked to field close and courageous at short-leg: I remember him plucking the ball right off the face of the bat, plunging to the ground to astonished gasps from the crowd – yes, a throwback indeed, for there were always crowds when my grandfather and I went to county cricket.

So there was much to admire. I used to steal the daily paper from my parents and scan the county cricket scoreboards, as inky-fingered boys had done for generations, and, like them, I found a brief taste of heaven or hell in what I found there as

I looked for Warwickshire, and for *M.J.K. Smith. He let me down, though, far too often. He let me down cruelly. I would note with dismay that he always seemed to score a century in matches that didn't matter, picnic occasions like Gentlemen v Players, the now obsolete fixture in which amateurs played the professionals in a genteel extension of the class war.

Smith had a devastating run of low scores in the 60s, vulnerable against pace at the start of an innings like so many other nearly-but-not-quiters. It saddened me that the heroes of my friends always did better than M.J.K. I was walking round the school playing field one day with my friends Stuart Barnett and Ian Hart, listening to the cricket on the radio. The year was 1965. England were playing New Zealand. Smith came out to bat, and was out for a duck, lbw to Richard Collinge. "A captain's innings!" Stuart mocked. Stuart was cruel; but then life is cruel, and so is sport. If it wasn't cruel, we wouldn't watch it. And if heroes didn't have the capacity to cause us pain, we wouldn't bother with them. I rather think I knew that then, but it wasn't much consolation.

2. Anita Lonsbrough

YOU ARE TOLD NEVER to meet your heroes. Such nonsense. Of course you should meet your heroes, if only for the disappointment. And anyway, I wasn't disappointed when I met Anita Lonsbrough, 44 years after I became aware of her heroic existence. I had been on nodding and halloing terms with her for some years before that, but I first had a proper conversation with her in Athens in 2004. She looked great: a statuesque lady of a certain age. She held herself beautifully: you'd know her at once as a former athlete if you had your wits about you. I was with my colleague from *The Times*, Craig Lord, swimming correspondent; Anita was filling the same role for the *Daily Telegraph*.

We had been covering the swimming at the Olympic Games for our newspapers, and having filed copy, we strolled out into the Olympic Park. The Athens park was big and bleak and punctuated with McDonalds. It was a place I never warmed to, despite the wonderful sport I saw there. But we were at least able to have a couple of beers in its underpopulated vastness – the Athenians never really took to their own Games – and we talked for a while. This gave me the opportunity to suggest to Anita that it was probably her fault that I was here in Athens, writing about the Olympic Games; her fault that I have spent most of my professional life in pursuit of the monstrous and glorious trivialities of sport; her fault that I have spent so many years enthralled by the question of heroes and heroism.

The Olympic Games of 1960 was the first sporting event that possessed me. It took me over. I had never been aware that such extraordinary things existed: that such wonder and glory could be experienced. I was nine that summer, and lost in the wonder of it, gazing at the black-and-white television in our sitting room in Streatham. Streatham is a place that needs its wonders pumped in from outside. From Rome, in great waves, there came the most extraordinary things I had ever seen, or ever been aware of. I had always sought my wonders in the natural world: here in the sitting room in Streatham was a revelation that humans were also capable of inspiring wonder and beauty and glory.

I discovered this without the delights of partisanship, for this was a disappointing Games for Britain. But disappointment is as vivid an experience as glory – or nearly. For it was when the joy of victory was added to the glories of the struggle that I knew sport would always hold me: and that was Anita's doing.

Swimmers have marvellous bodies: not ostentatiously muscled, not, when they are down to business, even remotely sexy. There is something sleek and purposeful and pared-down about a swimmer's body: a benign strength not intended to damage anyone. It is a very pure thing, a swimmer's body, almost literally other-worldly, for it has been trained and honed and polished to excel in water: in another element: in another world.

Anita was 19 when she competed at the Olympic Games in Rome. She took part in the 200 metres breaststroke. Black- and-white television, a grainy image, a hysterical commentator, the sight of eight grey swimming caps and the grey water churned into grey froth by all the grey arms and legs. Eight bow-waves advancing and retreating up and down the pool. The gasping faces, the heads appearing and disappearing in their own rhythm. It looks a trifle comical to see the event now, for swimming has changed as all sport has changed, but all the same, these people were the best in the world, and back then they all looked like gods. Rebecca Soni of the United States set a new world record for Anita's event, 2.20.22, at the Olympic Games of 2008; Anita's world record from Rome was 2.49.5, almost half a minute slower. But both swimmers had spent their lives preparing for a single moment – that is what the Olympics mean, that is why the Olympics provide the greatest test of them all. One difference, though. Soni was working as a professional swimmer, and Anita worked as a clerk in Huddersfield Town Hall.

Anita won. Of course she did. I remember the madness of the commentator, Anita's face lit up for ever in the beauty of victory. Her rival, Wiltrud Usel of West Germany, had come storming back over the last length, but Anita held on. Britain had won a gold medal, Anita had won a gold medal, I had won a gold medal. I tasted the joys of partisanship and victory, and marvelled that sport could bring such wonderful things.

Anita was the first woman to be made BBC Sports Personality of the Year, and at the Olympic Games in Tokyo in 1964, she was the first woman to carry the British flag in the opening ceremony. But I never thought that there was anything remotely odd about women doing great things. My mother, a feminist long before the term was invented, had made it clear that women could be admired with the same freedom as men could. It never seemed inappropriate to have a woman as a hero. Heroines are no different from heroes.

I also attended the Beijing Olympic Games of 2008, 48

years after Anita had won her gold medal. In all that time, no British woman had won an Olympic gold medal in the swimming pool. And there I was, sitting next to Craig, as we both covered the event for *The Times*. On Craig's other side sat Anita. I was there to write about the extraordinary Michael Phelps, who was to go on and win eight gold medals at the Games. But there was also a race, the 400 metres freestyle, in which a British swimmer had a chance for a medal. Rebecca Adlington might well get a bronze.

Bang. Off they swam. The two favourites, Katie Hoff of the United States and Federica Pellegrini of Italy, knew that they had the race between them. But which would it be? They sized each other up as the race unfolded. Each was reluctant to make a break and then get caught. And then, roaring past them, taking advantage of their fear, came the fearless Adlington, blasting through to the finish like a terrible judgement on timidity, and there were Craig and Anita on their feet, shouting her home and then embracing, and Anita's eyes glistening, mine too. I didn't know Anita well enough for hugging, but I think I touched her arm, or her shoulder, a movement to represent the hug that would have been out of place. She knew what I meant all right. "Too long," she said. "Too long."

Always meet your heroes, if you have a chance. And if you can, be with them at the moment when history turns and sets their greatest accomplishment into a newer and richer perspective. I realised at the swimming pool in Beijing that I had spent 48 years looking for heroes. Not long enough.

3. Don Thompson

I HAVE MEASURED OUT my life with heroes. We all do. Heroes people our lives, with their virtues and their vices, some complementing each other, others frankly contradicting the values our other heroes stand for. Take just a few of the heroes from my schooldays: Robin Hood, Odysseus, Ratty, Bagheera, Emma Peel, Lawrence of Arabia, Hank Marvin, Champion the Wonder Horse, John Lennon, Che Guevara, Ludwig van Beethoven, Stephen Dedalus, Modesty Blaise, David Attenborough and Reepicheep. You can't call this a pantheon, because that is a collection of gods, and heroes are quite different from gods. A classical scholar named Jeremy Mynott, a friend who is in the middle of translating Thucydides, has kindly coined a term that will do instead. Panheroikon: a collection of heroes.

I thought about writing a book about all these different kinds of heroes, comparing, say, M.J.K. Smith with Robin Hood and Anita Lonsbrough with Modesty Blaise. But the more I looked at the heroes of my life, the more vast and complex the subject became. Looking for heroes is like looking for stars at dusk.

The subject rapidly becomes too huge, too confusing, inchoate. It was clear that if I wanted to examine the notion of heroes and heroism, I must take a less pan-galactic view. Sport has always been my subject; I have written about it, mostly for *The Times*, for most of my grown-up life, so it's sporting heroes I have turned to. You might say that the provision of heroes is the basic point of sport. If sport didn't provide heroes, sport wouldn't command our imaginations.

Few people have had a less heroic aspect than Don Thompson, a slight figure in a funny hat who lived with his mum.

He was another hero of the 1960 Olympic Games: he won Britain's only other gold medal in Rome. I had grown aware, as the Games unfolded, that Britain was embarrassed by the shortage of medals. In particular, by the lack of gold medals in athletics. One by one, the sprinters and the middle-distance runners, the leapers and the chuckers, failed to bring Britain the success that once came Britain's way as a matter of course. But then came the 50-kilometre walk. Of all things, one might add.

I had no idea that such an event took place, or that the human frame was capable of walking so vast a distance. But they set off: I don't think I saw the beginning of the race. I certainly didn't see the middle of the race, because the technology for bringing the 49 mid-race kilometres to our screens simply didn't exist. As the race drew towards its conclusion, I found that I was watching – agog – an empty stadium. No athletes, just an expectant crowd and the voices of commentators gallantly busking it. The black-and-white image of the Stadio Olimpico – where I was to watch so many matches for *The Times* at the 1990 Football World Cup – was there on the television screen at 50 Hill House Road. Where were the walkers? And in what order did they walk?

There was a rumour, but no more than a rumour, that a British walker was doing well, that he was in the lead. But these sounded deeply untrustworthy. We had all been disappointed too many times: even me, a child new to sport. I learned about disappointment long before I learned about glory. I remember the wait, a long one. The grand stadium. The complete absence of action: and yet there was something enthralling about the stillness, the knowledge that a great struggle was taking place elsewhere, out of sight. As if this was a Greek play. And then the entrance. The entrance of the hero.

It must have looked a comic sight to some. Race-walking exists on the edge of farce at the best of times, and here, leading all and doing so by a distance, was a small, skinny figure, elbows working as if he was trying to play two violins at the same time, hips swaying like Marilyn Monroe on the train platform in *Some Like it Hot* – "like Jell-O on springs!" – wearing dark glasses in the dark, and an improvised Foreign Legion hat on his head. It was years later that I learned that he had got his mother to sew a handkerchief onto the back of a standard cap, because he was convinced that the heat was a tougher opponent than his flesh-and-blood ones.

Heat had already cost him one gold medal, and he didn't want it to cost him a second. Four years earlier, he had collapsed from dehydration at 45 kilometres at the Olympic Games in Melbourne. He was determined not to let this happen again, so he prepared for the heat with a glorious crackpot Heath-Robinson Wallace-and-Gromit dedication. He rigged up a heat-training system in the bathroom of his mum's house, carrying in boiling kettles and a Valor stove, bringing the temperature up beyond blood heat, to 100 degrees Fahrenheit. Here, he would exercise. He could only stand it for half an hour, because he got dizzy. He thought this was because of the heat: he didn't realise until years later that it was actually carbon monoxide poisoning. There was no thought of warm-weather training, as a modern athlete and medal hope would certainly take on. Thompson got no money for racing. He worked as an insurance clerk.

The legend of his makeshift training has become part of his hero's legacy. In truth he only used it for three half-hour sessions a week: "More about a boost to my confidence," he said. By doing this, he anticipated one of the standard tenets of sports psychology by about 30 years. He invented the notion of making friends with the stadium, of getting the place of competition on your side. It was this improvised mental preparation that gave him his edge. In the race, he pulled away from his rival, John Ljunggren of Sweden, and then put a despairing distance between them, reaching the stadium alone and completing a lap inside. Ljunggren had barely entered the stadium as Thompson elbowed and wiggled his way to the tape. The Italians liked him: the papers called him "*il topolino*", the little mouse.

And my imagination was caught by the unlikely triumph of an unlikely man in an unlikely event. I was infected by the beauty of walking, and have been ever since. In those days before paedophiliaphobia, I used to leave Hill House Road and go for long solitary walks about south London; trudges, I used to call them. Often I would march to the Crystal Palace mast and back. Sometimes I swung my elbows and wiggled my hips as I went, but I soon got bored with that. I wasn't really walking for sport. I wasn't really looking for speed and time, or even distance. I was walking for the sake of walking, and I have walked for the same reason ever since. I have walked when beset by troubles, I have walked to seek joy. I have walked miles of cliff-path in Cornwall, I have walked in the bush among the lions and the elephants in Africa, I have walked, sweating and much bitten, through rainforests; I have walked miles in New York and Venice and across

Suffolk where I live. I have learned that walking is the best way of understanding the place, of getting the world on your side.

And it began with Thompson. It began with a classic British eccentric with a mind fully engaged with the question of winning. He went on to become the oldest person ever to compete at full international level for Britain, taking part in a 200-kilometre event in 1991 at the age of 58.

Heroes don't have to be big or imposing or even spectacularly sane. They just have to be heroic: and heroism is a protean thing, never quite the same from individual to individual. A hero can wear a funny hat and walk a silly walk and live with his mother: but that doesn't stop him being heroic. Not if the person watching is capable of being reached by his heroism.

4. Abebe Bikila

THE SAME CITY, the same wait, the same year, the same Olympic Games. The Appian Way in Rome in 1960, and once again the action somewhere else, but getting nearer every second, with every unseen footfall. The circumstances that had already brought me one hero were about to bring me another. It held all the mystery of classical drama, obeying the Aristotelian rules of the unity of action, so that the great events take place off-stage, never seen, but are instead reported by a chorus of unreliable aspect.

This time it was the marathon. I don't need to specify that this was the men's marathon: it would be 24 years before women were considered strong enough to run 26-plus miles. Back then, running so colossal a distance was in itself an extraordinary thing: a thing only the most exceptional – and mad – athletes even considered. To complete a marathon was a matter reserved for the most remarkable people on the planet. How they did it was in itself a mystery. After all, we never saw them.

I had never seen a marathon, not even the finish of one. I just sat there marvelling at the idea that people – unseen, off-stage – were in the process of running without stopping for more than two hours. They were all heroes, that was plain. But who was going to be the supreme athlete, the greatest man of them all, the hero among the heroes? Who would lead the rest to the finish on the Appian Way? It was a blank page, filled in by a child's imagination, made marvellous by the limitations of technology.

But it was more marvellous than I could have imagined, and I had an imagination well fed by *The Jungle Books* and the *Chronicles of Narnia* and by Robin Hood and by Lawrence of

Arabia. He appeared before us: lithe, African, barefoot. He was like an emissary from the Lost World, from King Solomon's Mines, from Shangri-La: from all the boyhood books of lost kingdoms, those kingdoms filled with great and noble people well outside the common run. This was Abebe Bikila. He was a member of the bodyguard of Haile Selassie, the King of Ethiopia. His father was a shepherd and he had no shoes. But he was faster and better than everyone in the world who took shoes for granted and my heart rejoiced in the glory of it all, in the mad exoticism of it all. In those distant times, I had not often come across people with different coloured skin from my own; Streatham had yet to go multicultural. I remember an Asian girl in my class called Shada Bhamel, for whom I had a sly passion; a black boy who joined the school later who was popular. Being a child, it never occurred to me that people with darker skins were inferior, or for that matter, greatly different. But I felt a difference all right when I had this transcendent vision of Bikila, running to the finish in the Roman night on his own African feet. I was conscious of superiority: the superiority of Bikila over everybody else. It was obvious at once that he was a truly exceptional being: one who really was on a different plane from the rest of the world. I was conscious of the arrival of a hero.

This was a child's view: but a glorious one for all that. I was eager for heroes: for a child, having heroes is one of the ways in which we grow up. We learn by finding people who please, who impress, who amaze, who tell us big things about the world. A child without a history of heroes is a child who has learned nothing. And I, genuinely innocent of racism, for this was not something I had encountered, at home or anywhere else, was given this first, this glorious experience of a non-white person in the form of unambiguous heroism.

Bikila had been picked out when his country employed a Swedish coach, Onni Niskanen, to identify and train a team of runners, so that Ethiopia might look good before the world at the Olympic Games. But Bikila was not one of the stars of this programme. He came into the Ethiopian Olympic team late in the day, because one of the more fancied runners broke a leg playing football. Bikila did, in fact, own a pair of running shoes. Adidas gave him these shoes before the competition, but he wasn't happy in them. They didn't fit, he said. So he discarded them before the start, and ran barefoot, as he had done in training.

He kept with his chief rival until 500 metres from the finish and then put his barefoot on the throttle and left him for dead. It was years before people realised that the combination of a carbohydrate-heavy diet and altitude training was the ideal preparation for distance running: but it was the way Bikila had lived all his life. All the same, it's one thing having an advantage, it's quite another making it work for you. That requires the ability to seize your day. I suspect I knew that even then.

It was the first Olympic gold medal won by a black African. Africa has haunted me all my life. I have made many trips there, mostly to Zambia, in search of the most wonderful wildlife on the planet. I have made friends there; I have written a novel set in an African national park. Perhaps it all began with the entry of this bare-foot, slight man and those strong, bony East African features, winning against the backdrop of the imperial splendours of Rome.

That was not the end of his story. Bikila ran the marathon at the Olympic Games in Tokyo four years later – but only just. It was 40 days before the race was due to start when he felt a pain. He tried to run through it, but couldn't. Not surprising: it was appendicitis. He had the operation, and started jogging in the hospital yard. He made the start line: made the finish too, winning by a distance, burning off the competition at 30 kilometres and running the last ten alone. No one could touch him. This time he wore shoes. After he finished, he performed a series of vigorous warming-down exercises to show how full of running he was. "I could have run another ten kilometres," he said. I remember the joy of seeing his remembered face, entering the awaiting stadium, the glorious cheek of those exercises, the wonderful self-delight of victory, of being the best, the very best, the best ever. Africa, the underdog continent, was for once, briefly, at the world's summit.

Bikila was promoted to corporal for his achievements, and was given a car, a VW Beetle. Some years later, he was involved in an accident in this vehicle, and was paralysed from the waist down. He took up archery. He died in 1973 of a cerebral haemorrhage.

5. Bobby Charlton

EVERY STORY IS A demonstration of the way things change. Sometimes a hero suffers or undergoes change, sometimes he brings change about. Sometimes he goes into a phone box and emerges with a cape; sometimes he sees a ghost and vows to avenge his father's death. In some stories a hero takes command. He makes one decisive act, slays the dragon or his father, and things can never be the same again.

In many stories, the hero slays the monster or fulfils a quest. As a result, it is not just the hero who is changed. The entire world is changed for the better, light banishes the darkness, and sweetness, prosperity and joy take over the world. Beowulf slays Grendel and at once, everything in life is improved out of all recognition. Such a hero's deeds go far beyond himself. By means of his huge and extraordinary nature, he labours for the entire world, for all the good people. By dint of his actions, his remarkable skills and his truly exceptional nobility of nature, he makes life better for us all. Night ends: eternal winter becomes spring: the time of sickness has ended: Jack shall have Jill, nought shall go ill, the man shall have his mare again and all shall be well. Bobby Charlton was that kind of hero. Just for one goal, one goal that slew the dragon despair and unleashed a monster called hope.

"Let's run and see what happens." That's what Charlton says he told himself as the Mexican defence retreated in front of him. The year was 1966. England were playing their second match in the World Cup against Mexico. The tournament had begun in a desperately disappointing fashion, with England in a goalless draw against the depressingly negative Uruguay team. All the pre-tournament hopes vanished in a terrible douche of reality. England were simply not good enough, never even looked like scoring, who do they think they're kidding, we were fools to think they would do any good, we don't play real football in this country, it's all kick and hope, the sophisticated nations like Italy, like Brazil, that's where real football is played, we just don't have what it takes, not at this level.

These things are particularly dismaying when you're young. You don't have the experience to know that people love to talk up the gloom, especially where the national football team is concerned. For me, watching in the sitting room in Streatham, it was the most desperate disappointment. I felt such an idiot for having hoped. And yet, when the second match came around and England lined up against Mexico, I felt a treacherous rekindling of hope. Fool, fool. For Mexico played the same stifling game as Uruguay, and it seemed clear that England would never score, still less advance in the tournament. It was horrible, it was miserable. It was also football, though I didn't know much about football. Mine was not a footballing family. My father is from Wigan; he loves rugby league and cricket; football meant nothing to him. I watched the World Cup unilaterally, fighting for the right to do so. In those days, football wasn't much seen on television. For years it was restricted to the annual national feast day of the FA Cup final, and the occasional international. Football's rhythms, its capricious nature, its essential dynamic, its extensive range of possibilities – all these things were unknown to me.

"The man who made it possible was Roger Hunt," Charlton said in the volume of his autobiography called *My England Years*, ghosted with wonderful sympathy by my old friend James Lawton. Hunt made a strong and elaborate decoy run, drew the defence and the match opened for Charlton. "I was still asking, when is somebody going to come to me?" Nobody did. So Charlton, now in shooting range, shot.

It was the most marvellous goal I have ever seen. I had no idea that a goal could be scored at such range, that a ball could travel so far and so fast. Maybe 25 yards. Maybe even 30. Well, let's be realistic: maybe 50 yards, maybe 100. Well, the ball seemed to travel the entire length of Streatham High Road, past the common, past Streatham Station, past St Leonard's Church, past Pratt's, past the library, past the cinema, and on towards Streatham Hill and the 137 bus stop.

It was glorious, ineffably glorious, a goal that changed reality, a goal that brought hope back into the world. Has a ball ever been struck so sweetly? Charlton's modest assessment is otherwise, but he said: "I do like to think that no goalkeeper in the world would have stopped it."

With that one extraordinary goal, a nation of atheists became a nation of believers. From that moment, England's progress towards victory acquired a glorious inevitability. That goal changed everything. Like a drug, it entirely altered your point of view. On England marched: past France and the row about Nobby Stiles, past Argentina and the "animals", past Portugal and Eusebio, and at the last, past West Germany and the goal that the linesman gave: and it all came from that one goal, that thing of beauty, flying like a beautiful bird.

Charlton did many things in football apart from scoring that goal. But nothing he did compares with it, not for me. My friend Ian thought otherwise, believing that everything Charlton touched was a thing of perfection. He even tried to convince me that Charlton wasn't bald: "It's just his hair is so blond you can't see it on television." Charlton was awarded 106 caps for England, he won the European Cup for Manchester United in 1968, he was a great player and a man of great decency. But we all know that.

For me, everything that mattered about Charlton is concerned with that one moment, that one strike, that one flight. One act, one deed, one moment: and nothing was the same afterwards. And I knew then that the impossible was always possible. That one person – one hero – can in one moment change the world.

6. Vibart

WE USED TO WATCH showjumping. It was the only sport we watched as a family. There used to be showjumping on prime-time television, every day for a week, a couple of times a year, and it was compulsive viewing, not just for us, but for the nation. If that seems like a despatch from a bygone age, that's because it is. David Broome won the BBC Sports Personality of the Year in 1960: yes, the most popular and well-thought-of athlete in the country was a showjumper. Mostly, when people talk of Golden Ages, it is nothing but nostalgic nonsense and a disinclination to deal with the present. But the 60s really were the Golden Age of Showjumping.

The strength of televised showjumping across that decade was in its continuity. Year after year, the same riders would enter the indoor arenas at Earl's Court and Wembley, and – here is the crucial point – they would be riding the same horses. Rider and horse were inseparable. There was Anneli Drummond-Hay on Merely-a-Monarch, David Broome on Mr Softee, Harvey Smith on Harvester, Marion Coakes on Stroller: everything about the sport was the celebration of a bond. There were foreign riders to spice things up: Alwin Schockemohle and the Italian cavalry officer, Major Raimondo d'Inzeo, in his dashing uniform. There was the drawling upper-class voice of the commentator, Dorian Williams, hilariously partisan: "Be careful, Harvey!" "Schockemohle sew lucky thar!"

The drama would play itself out before us: one tightly-bonded pair following another. It was unthinkable that any of these riders would ever sit on another horse. It would have been a betrayal. And the gasps and sighs as a pole fell, and the roar at the conclusion of a clear round: these things would be part of my life, many years later, when I competed in equestrian sports. I too have heard the sigh, not given by thousands but at least by tens; I too have heard, if not the roar, then at least the murmur of approval and the clatter of a few clapping hands.

But we were not a horsey family. If anything, we were opposed to horsey people. We were media pinkoes, from the art-struck middle classes; we were townies who found the idea of the country life barbaric and hilarious. My parents mildly despised horsiness in all its forms. But we were united in our love for showjumping on television. And the horse that I loved best was Vibart. He was huge. His mother was a Clydesdale, beasts bred to pull farmers' carts, the heavier the better. Vibart's father was a thoroughbred, but Vibart never gave the impression of speed and sleekness. He was all about bulk and power. He was a horse of a particularly overwhelming kind.

He could jump all right; he could jump with what looked like uncontrollable power: certainly, the power never seemed to be fully under the control of either horse or rider. Then, when he reached the apex of his jump, he would inexplicably lash out with his back feet. Occasionally he would double-barrel a top rail – absolutely middle it – and send the damn thing for miles. As a result, every mighty leap was fraught with danger. Most great showjumping horses have a slightly finicky streak: they lift their forelegs and then their hindlegs over the fences as if they fear contamination from the slightest touch. But Vibart would charge at them, take wing and then lash out with absent-minded venom.

His rider was Andrew Fielder, a man who always looked a trifle overwhelmed. He seemed mild yet curiously unworried by the madcap beast beneath him. He wore spectacles and didn't in the least look like a man prone to wild risks. There was nothing dashing and devil-may-care about him: he delegated all that to the horse. The first time Fielder saw Vibart, Vibart took a couple of fences and then stood bolt upright: a rear, that most frightening of equine vices. For Fielder it was an instant attraction. He was 14 at the time, and had already done all his growing: he was a briefly freakish 5 ft 11. When he rode ponies, he tended to knock down jumps with his feet. He needed a proper horse. Perhaps he overcompensated. Vibart was 17 hands and two inches – all but six foot at the shoulder – and a 50-50 mixture of vice and talent. As a boy's first proper horse, Vibart was a ludicrous choice. But Fielder was greatly talented: and had the right understanding, one that perhaps a grown man would have lacked. Fielder always worked with the horse, rather than against.

Later on, after the horsey life had claimed me, I grew to understand a little of what I had seen. In Fielder's mildness lay his strength. Had he attempted to fight the horse and insisted on his own way with every stride, he would have lost. The horse might have jumped, but he certainly would not have put his heart into jumping. There would have been no success. Fielder's talent was in his egolessness. His achievement came from his refusal to dominate. His technique was based on generosity, sympathy, understanding. I have ridden some overwhelming horses in my time – at an infinitely lower level of competition, I must stress – and I have found my own response much the same: you want a fight? You won't get one here. Rather, you'll be quietly persuaded. To make a team. To form a bond.

Fielder and Vibart were astonishingly successful, given Vibart's harum-scarum nature. Right from the beginning, Fielder's calm tolerance brought the best from the horse. There was a litany of prizes and ribbons and achievements: perhaps the summit was the fortnight in 1967 when Vibart and Fielder helped Britain to win the Nations Cup at Aachen, then won the Aachen Grand Prix for individual combinations, and after that, the Hamburg Jumping Derby. The following year they won the Leading Showjumper of the Year class at the Horse of the Year Show – the third time they had done so – and I was there at home in Streatham to revel in it.

Can a horse really be a hero? Isn't that rather sentimental? Absurdly anthropomorphic? No doubt the answer to all three questions is yes. Vibart stood for strength, power, ability: but he also stood for eccentricity, for self-imposed handicap, for a cavalier disdain for convention. He went at a showjumping course like a misfit: and yet – rarely, but gloriously – he showed that he was better than his prim and proper, readily controllable opponents.

Vibart was the maverick who refused to do anything in the normal, accepted way, and yet had so much talent he could beat them anyway: who could not thrill at such an idea? Vibart was a rebel: and yet he could beat all the non-rebels at their own game. Intoxicating stuff, for a boy moving into his teens in the 1960s. And yet the deeper meaning of Vibart, the one I was to learn much later, was in the personality of the rider, in Fielder's mild bespectacled face. Fielder made it clear that what matters is not dominance, but partnership. Not the control, but the letting-go. Riding Vibart was a fight all right: but it was a fight that they both won. Is that what partnership means? Is that what heroism means?

7. George Best

THERE ARE TIMES WHEN the adoption of a hero involves a moral choice. Not all heroes represent the obviously good, nor do they all obligingly line up against the obviously bad. True, you are not going to side with the Sheriff of Nottingham against Robin Hood, or for that matter, if English, with Franz Beckenbauer against Bobby Charlton. At occasions like these, partisanship takes on the illusion of moral force.

Choosing George Best was difficult for me, at least at first. I know that this looks ludicrous now. It is an established fact of footballing history that everyone loved Best. Everyone who was there remembers being in love with his skill, his style, his folly and his glory. But this is a false memory: the rewriting of history. Best did not unite. Best divided. Best met with bitter opposition. For as long as he was a genuinely great player, he was loathed every bit as much as he was loved.

The idea that the 60s were one long party, one long celebration of love, is something that arrived a long time after the 60s ended. It was promulgated by those who at first stood wholeheartedly against the forces of change and freedom, and then half-heartedly tagged along with these ideas when it was too late to change them. Much later, they firmly believed they had been in the vanguard all along.

The 60s were a time of opposition, and football represented this as much as anything. Mostly, it did so through the person of Best. If you look up some of his great moments, you will see that this is true. Best was a man of a thousand skills, but the greatest of these was his ability to ride tackles. If you watch his high-speed slaloming runs at defence, you will see that in many, he is kicked, hard, three or four times, within a few seconds. These days, each one of these assaults would be regarded as a foul. The kicked player would go down in a heap at the first hack, the kicker would get a yellow card, and the game would restart from a free kick. But Best played in a different landscape. It is often said that Best played by different rules: it was quite literally the case. The point is that the rules were all against him.

Players were allowed to kick him. There was even a sense in which they were encouraged to do so. There was a school of thought that held that it was morally appropriate for strong, disciplined, short-haired players to chastise Best for the liberties he took, the liberties he represented. But Best didn't go down. There would have been no point. With astonishing balance, he kept his feet and maintained his speed; in this manner, he would beat one man after another, and fire his shot at goal. It looks absolutely nothing like modern football: the kicking is no longer permitted and the skill to defeat the kickers is no longer necessary. Best always said that clogging defenders never worried him, because "they weren't much good at it". At times he would taunt them, like a matador: hold the ball at his feet and beckon them towards him: come on, have a go, kick me. Then, with impossible grace, in a manner impossible to predict because he had so many tricks and was so perfectly two-footed, the clogger would be left behind, vowing to get him next time.

There was an occasion when Best, playing for Northern Ireland rather than his club, Manchester United, was sent off. He had been kicked to the ground so many times, ending up in the mud of one of those eternal 60s quagmire pitches. He turned to the referee and flicked the mud from his hands, to say enough was surely enough. He was right. The referee sent him off for throwing mud. Effectively, Best was sent off for being kicked. Many people said that it served him right.

Football was caught between generations, like everything else at the time. But sport tends to show such matters in dramatic form, and when things are shown in dramatic form, you find the dramatic phenomenon known as the hero. Much of football was still under the influence of austerity and wartime, highlighting above all else the values of discipline and obedience. This view is caught in Hunter Davies's classic, *The Glory Game*, which tells of a year with Tottenham Hotspur. Davies's portrayal of the assistant manager, Eddie Bailey, is unforgettable. As Spurs were about to play Nantes: "Right, bayonets on… Over the top. Let's have you." No one could associate Best with outdated military values.

Best offered a choice. We could judge him by these outdated values, or by a new set of values, values not yet clearly laid down. For quite a time, I wasn't sure myself which way to go. My parents found Best a mainly comic character. Football was alien to them, but Best was not a figure they approved of. The prevailing tone, in newspapers and on television, was distinctly ambiguous: they fed on his celebrity, but often with disapproval. There were many who thought that Best represented everything that was wrong in English football, everything that was wrong "in Britain today", a phrase much bandied about at the time.

One of the problems was Best's extraordinary gracefulness, his too-apparent beauty. There was something feminine about him. Many deplored this unmanliness, or perhaps the confusion it provoked within them. To confuse things further, Best seemed to have made it his mission to take the traditional masculine obsessions to new levels of extremity. Football, birds and booze: has anyone ever pursued all three with such dedication? But the long hair, the hip-flicking grace, the sinuous running: all of this disturbed people greatly. There was something voluptuous about his skill, and Best said, in a book he did with Michael Parkinson, that he got sexually aroused before matches. There was always something uncomfortable about Best: there is always something uncomfortable about extreme talent. Perhaps there should always be something uncomfortable about any hero.

I had yet to make my choices. I had yet to make my choice about the 60s, about where I stood, about what mattered. I had yet to establish a role, a style. Like everyone else in Upper Five Arts, I tied my tie very neatly in a half-Windsor knot, wore cuff-links and combed my hair frenziedly; but I also wore illegal elastic-sided shoes, read strange books and listened to strange music. In short, I didn't know which way to jump.

Best was part of the process that gave me direction. As people began to gloat at the failure of Best, his falling away from triumph, so I began to understand the point of him. He was European Footballer of the Year in 1968, the year Manchester United won the European Cup. The decisive goal came at the beginning of extra time, when Best took the ball 25 yards, went round two defenders and slid the ball past the goalkeeper.

But from this high point, the descent was sharp. And now I was with him. I could see the artistry in Best, I could begin to see that the flaws of his excessive nature were what made him a great footballer, I could see why Carl Jung (encountered in one of those strange books) said that the task of a psychologist was to allow men of genius to help their neuroses.

Football is not an art, but Best made it look like one. Your opponents do not cooperate with you, but Best made it seem as if they were taking part in a glorious ritual dance, one designed to showcase the talents of Best. And eventually, I made my choice. I was for liberty, I was for artistry, I was for excess, I was for joy. I was for Best.

8. Garry Sobers

WHAT IS IT LIKE, I wonder – to be absolutely brilliant at everything you turn to? As if you couldn't help yourself. As if brilliance was your default state. You just pick something up: and you're brilliant at it. If you ever found the answer, then I suppose you'd know what it was like to be Garry Sobers. He was a cricketer who could do everything cricket asked of anybody, and do it brilliantly. It has been said that Dante was the last man in history who knew everything that his society had learned. Sobers was cricket's Dante: the summary of all its skills. He was a great batsman, of course, but he began his career as a specialist bowler, batting at nine. He was a left-arm seamer who sent down fast-medium swingers. But he was also a spin bowler: master of that almost contradictory discipline of finger spin. And he could also bowl a completely different style of spinner: offering left-arm wrist-spin, which cricketers call "chinamen". This delivery was, of course, varied with a googly.

As a fielder there was no one to touch him, no matter where he was fielding: Bostick-fingered when catching close to the bat, athletic and with a bazooka-arm when fielding deep. He really could do everything: and what's more, in the course of a single Test match, he usually did do everything, and did it all with brilliance. I have found no record of him keeping wicket, but had he ever done so, he'd have been one of the finest wicketkeepers that ever pulled on a gauntlet. Anything that cricket asked, Sobers answered.

I stumbled on a line that sums up his cricketing skills. Dave Liverman wrote it in a few brief paragraphs on the Cricinfo website: "As a batsman he was great, as a bowler merely superb." It's worth noting that he excelled at every other sport he tried: as a teenager he played football for Barbados, as a goalkeeper, and he played basketball for the national team After he retired from cricket, he was captain of golf for Barbados.

It was 1963, and I was 12. I was now more aware of the existence of different races and cultures: they were increasingly part of south London life. Streatham is just a few bus stops from Brixton: go past Streatham Hill Station, cross the South Circular at Christchurch Road, and continue down the hill. Brixton was a foreign country. You could buy yams in the market. You could turn off the main road and seldom see a white face. I was told a story by a friend of my parents about the time he had gone to the top of a bus that passed through Brixton: his was the only white face. The conductor addressed him, in broad Jamaican: "Dr Livingstone, ah presume." Brixton was loud with Jamaican patois: for a generation, this was one of the great and omnipresent voices of London. I would pay my own bus fares to a West-Indian bus conductor, and he would accept my request in a voice that you only hear today when Lennie Henry does his mum. I can still hear the litany of the station announcer on Clapham Junction Station, as I waited for my train home from school: Balham Streatham Common NARbury Tarntoneath Sellarse Easeroydon Sarth-Croydon ParlyOak Sparleon Coulsdin Narth.

So yes, I was middle class, and mostly came across black people when they were doing menial jobs. We didn't know much about people with different-coloured skin at school. Most of the follies and idiocies of my youth I am prepared to take in my stride: I am not ashamed of having once been young. But the jokes from those days fill me with cold horror: jokes about blacks and enormous cocks and limited intelligence. We told them, as it were, in inverted commas, to show that we were so far removed from anything you could call prejudice that we were even able to make a joke of prejudice. We were fooling ourselves. These jokes were a symptom of our total confusion about race: our failure to understand, from complete lack of personal experience, the ways in which people from different backgrounds, cultures and races are like us and for that matter, not like us. Bewildering times.

So when the West Indies cricket team arrived in this country, there was a sense of thrilling exoticism. The late spring felt like a voyage of discovery. The West Indies came to England that year when I turned 12, and again three years later. Both times they were superb, both times they beat the best that England could throw at them, both times Sobers was the nonpareil. He was everything an English cricketer – everything, it seemed to me then, that an English person could ever want to be.

In that first series England fought back with a heroic win in the third Test, inspired by the great English bowler Fred Trueman. But Sobers set things aright in the next match: a century in the first innings, a half-century in the next, and taking three wickets as England fell to defeat. He was even better in 1966. Unbeatable. Unplayable. He scored 161 in the first Test, 163 in the second, 174 in the fourth. In the third he took four wickets in the first innings; in the fourth, eight wickets in the match. He scored 81 in the fifth.

I have a sort of black-and-white memory of him: a single moving snapshot, like the ones in the Harry Potter books, one that seems to encompass not a single stroke but every stroke he every played. I remember, above all, his phenomenal speed. Not speed like a sprinter, though he had that too, of course. It was speed of hand and eye and foot: he was cat-footed at the crease, hands like a whip, and he had apparently a hundred or so possible strokes to play at any one ball: a vast range of options made possible because everyone else was playing in slow-motion.

To start praising a black man, still worse black people in general, because of a gift for sport, is dangerous, getting close to that ancient crumb of praise: they gotta great sense of rhythm. And we were prone to terrible errors of understanding in those times. But it was plain that Sobers was showing something more than physical strength, or even great hand-and-eye coordination: things that can be patronisingly described as "natural" talent. It was clear that Sobers had more: call it great mind–eye coordination, if you like. True-man said that no batsman ever worked out a bowler faster than Sobers.

Sobers was not a role model. He was much more important than that. I had no notion of trying to be like Sobers: his was a talent too remote for emulation. Rather, Sobers affected my mind, helped me to think straight. Here was a man manifestly black of face, but with talents – and not just physical talents – that all eleven of the eleven greatest English cricketers could only envy. Sobers was the role model no one could use as a model. He taught us boys from our nice school in south London a few things, too. About humanity.

9. Bob Beamon

DURING THE COURSE OF the Ashes summer of 2009, I had an argument in print with Mike Atherton on the subject of Andrew Flintoff. I said that Flintoff was a great cricketer. Atherton, former England cricket captain and cricket correspondent of *The Times*, said that Flintoff was nothing of the kind. He wasn't consistent; his deeds didn't pass the test of longevity. Greatness, in short, needed to be set in the context of time. I said that Flintoff had, on occasions, touched greatness, and that was enough. Atherton said no: greatness had to involve sustained achievement. Greatness cannot be measured without factoring in a substantial period of time.

I had what I, at least, considered an unanswerable argument. Beamon.

Bob Beamon achieved greatness in a single bound. That is the literal truth. At the Olympic Games in Mexico City in 1968, his single bound covered 8.90 metres, 29 feet 2 ½ inches. It was a long-jump of a length no one had dreamed of. The record had been broken 13 times since 1901, by an average of 6 cm a time, or a couple of inches. Beamon broke the record by 55 cm, by 21¾ inches, and the record stood for 23 years.

It was a devastating revelation of human potential. It was a leap beyond the possible. It was a form of flight. I watched the jump on television, and couldn't believe what I saw: it seemed that the man would never come down. It was like one of those dreams in which you step into the air and travel wherever you wish, simply by means of the will. Gravity becomes vulnerable to the mind, leaving the dreamer floating, triumphant, ecstatic, fulfilled as never before.

In a couple of seconds, Beamon turned the world up-side down. He landed with two feet together, and took four bunny-hops out of the pit. He thought he'd made a pretty good jump, but he had no idea what he had achieved. It took a while for him to find out, too, because he had jumped beyond the optical measuring device. They had to measure his jump the old-fashioned way, with a tape measure. Eventually the result was read out: 8.90 metres. That meant nothing to Beamon: he was used to feet and inches. But then came the figure that registered: let's have it again: 29 feet 2½ inches. Beamon heard – and passed out. He collapsed in shock, and, shaken by a sudden nausea, he had to be helped by his teammates: "I guess I had a fainting fit."

I have been in the Olympic stadium when a world record had fallen, and it is like nothing else in sport: a stunned silence, a huge roar, a euphoric sense that we have all shared in a moment of imperishable significance. We are more than witnesses: we are participants in a miracle. What must it have been like, in that stadium in Mexico City, when the greatest record-breaking achievement in Olympic history happened before your eyes?

It was wonderful enough back in Streatham. It was as if everything perfect had been assembled especially for this jump. Mexico City is 2,240 metres above sea level, or 7,349 feet. Competitors in the explosive events got extra value for every ounce of effort, while those in the endurance events struggled to get a decent lungful of oxygen. The greatest detonation of them all was Beamon. He also had a following wind of two metres a second, precisely the legal limit. Beamon was feeling calm and peaceful: "I didn't hear anybody."

And he got everything right for just one jump. For just one occasion in his life – the one moment for which all other moments had been preparation – he found perfection: of speed, of coordination, of timing. He hit the board and flew, he hung in the air, he hit the sandpit and bunny-hopped out of it. And found greatness. He was aged 22: and he had done everything he could possibly do. So there was a touch of sadness about this moment of supreme achievement: a certainty that neither he, nor anybody else, stood any chance at all of following that. There was an element of freakishness about it: also an element of genuine greatness. One moment: one only: and he got it right. He got it perfect.

Beamonesque. The expression that has crept into sport. When any performer in any sport does something so colossal that he not only makes but seems to subvert history: that's Beamonesque. When any athlete does something so immense, something that nobody has ever done before and it seems that nobody will ever do again – that's Beamonesque.

When Beamon took off he was a very good track and field athlete. When he landed he was one of the seminal figures in sporting history, and with it, one of the great metaphorical figures of our time. Sport is the great myth-maker of modern life, and Beamon, with a single act, became one of its great heroes. He was – is – the man who had a single chance to work a miracle, and did so. As such, like Oedipus, like Odysseus, like the man painting the Forth Bridge, he has become part of the way we understand the world. That gives him heroic status. And – perhaps quite incidentally – he is a good man.

Beamon had known difficult times, times of deprivation. He was brought up in New York by his grandmother after his mother died when he was eight months old. He ran with gangs and found trouble. But he liked track and field, and got the taste for the hard work that this discipline requires. He got an athletic scholarship to the University of Texas, El Paso, but was suspended when he refused to compete against Brigham Young University because of their racist policies. He was a black man in 60s America: he knew about strife and upheaval and changing times. He went on to live a life committed to civic charities and urban youth.

But like Jesse Owens before him, he showed the world a greatness that anybody but a blockhead could understand. He got it right for a single moment only: but it was enough. Klaus Beer of East Germany was second with a jump of 8.19 metres. Igor Ter-Ovanesyan of the Soviet Union was next to go after Beamon: "I was ashamed to jump," he said.

Beamon never again jumped as far as 27 feet. It was another 12 years before any athlete cleared 28 feet again. Beamon's record was finally broken by Mike Powell 23 years later, at the World Athletics Championships in Tokyo in 1991. That record still stands; Beamon's mark is still the second longest jump of all time.

Beamon gave us something momentary, something utterly ephemeral, something that seemed then and seems now to be set about with eternity. He became a hero in an eyeblink. "I felt that once I did it, why do it again?"

10. Tommie Smith

IT'S HARD TO FIND many links between my two heroic Smiths of the 60s, between M.J.K. and Tommie. There's the name. And then there's me. And that's it. M.J.K. was conventional in all save his leg-side emphasis. He was a man of blazers and glasses; white, middle class, English, conservative, precisely the man you'd expect to propose to Miss Joan Hunter Dunn after the dance at the golf club.

Tommie was black, American, a rebel and a martyr. Martyr meaning, of course, witness. Tommie Smith didn't sacrifice his life: only his professional life, only his career, only his chance to make money, only his chance to be a hero for the American Establishment. Instead, he chose to be a hero for American rebels, and by chance, a hero for me. And for many other white middle-class people who were leaving childhood behind.

My own taste in heroes was changing – though I suppose the basic requirement for heroism is essentially the same, in any age, at any stage in life. That is to say courage. That is to say, the willingness to stand out from the rest. But Tommie Smith turned against the framework that traditionally provides the modern world with heroes. He turned against sport. By doing so, he became one of sport's eternal icons.

Smith won the 200 metres at the 1968 Olympic Games in Mexico City in 19.83 seconds. Peter Norman of Australia was second, John Carlos, also of the United States, was third. But of course, it wasn't the race that anyone remembers. I have no recollection of it at all. It was the medal ceremony that became part of history: part of the mythology of sport: a great emblem of America, the 60s, the civil rights movement, of protest, of freedom, of hope, of despair, of defiance. The victorious Smith knew he could only lose when he made his protest: but he also knew that it was more glorious to lose in this way than to win a gold medal on the track.

It was the awful dignity of it all that was so powerful. Yesterday's rebels become today's heroes: the protest on the medal podium by Smith and Carlos was so calm, so still, that it was as if they made themselves a living sculpture. Now the moment has been recreated in a non-living sculpture: you can see it on the campus of San Jose State University: the moment captured unmoving and 22 feet high.

There was something solemn and meaningful going on; I knew that even before they reached the podium to receive their medals. You could read it in the firm, set faces of Smith and Carlos. I didn't notice that both were wearing black socks and no shoes, to represent black poverty. I saw that Smith was wearing a black scarf, but I didn't know it was for black pride, and thought nothing of it. They each wore a single black glove, Smith the right, Carlos the left. This was because Carlos had forgotten his own gloves: but that somehow added to the perfection of this piece of deliberate symbolism. It was Norman, the silver medal-winner, who suggested they wore a glove each.

All three accepted their medals. Then, as the American national anthem rolled out across the stadium, slowly, calmly, unstoppably – though something inside made me want to shout No! Don't do it! – each man raised a single black-gloved fist. Heads bowed, fists solemnly lifted at the end of an extended arm, as the sacred tune of the land of the free filled the stadium and washed into millions of homes across the world. And I, who was playing at being a rebel myself, was filled with awe, with horror, with pity, for I, though a million miles from being worldly wise, could guess the trouble that this mad measured gesture would bring on them. The stadium rang with boos.

My mother, no friend of extreme politics or of self-conscious rebellion, was impressed despite herself. "That was the American national anthem. If you have reservations about it, you are entitled to express them." This was, at the domestic level, almost as big a surprise as the protest itself: and in my mother's unexpected response we can see the sculptural beauty of the protest. "If I win, I am an American, not a black American," Smith said. "But if I did something bad, then they would say I am a negro. We are black and we are proud of being black. Black America will understand what we did tonight." So, in a small way, did a white middle-class boy in Streatham, by now conscious of the bitter oppositions of the 60s.

Smith and Carlos had isolated themselves. Avery Brundage, autocratic president of the International Olympic Committee, was outraged. At first, the United States team refused to suspend the athletes, but Brundage said that if they didn't, he would suspend the entire American team. So the United States Olympic Committee capitulated. The IOC described the actions of Smith and Carlos as "a deliberate and violent breach of the fundamental principles of Olympic Sport".

This from an organisation that held the 1936 Games in Berlin, amid the swirl of swastikas and Nazi salutes. The fact is that the Olympic Games have always been political. To sort people by nation is by definition a political act. The Olympic Games became an unambiguous extension of the Cold War, with Games in Moscow in 1980 and Los Angeles in 1984, each event solemnly boycotted by the opposite side. The Games were held in Beijing in 2008, and China tried to make the occasion one of nationalist triumphalism. The Olympic Games cannot help but be political.

Both athletes inevitably suffered for their protest. They were hated, and received death threats, which extended to their families. Their careers in athletics were more or less over at a stroke. Both went on to play American football and both eventually worked in education, Smith as track coach at Oberlin College, Carlos coaching track and field at Palm Springs High School. Even Norman, who wore an Olympic Project for Human Rights badge in support, was vilified by the conservative Australian media.

America, embarrassed before the world, reacted strongly. *Time* magazine reported the protest as a cover story, under the words that parodied the Olympic motto: "Angrier, Nastier, Uglier." But the Civil Rights movement marched on – time waits for no magazine – and the protest of Smith and Carlos has become sanctified as a moment of great American courage. The fact that it was great anti-American courage is a contradiction that America appears to have taken in its stride. Smith and Carlos, hated and reviled, are now American heroes. All it took was time: that, and the courage of many others besides these two athletes.

But Smith and Carlos were heroes for me in 1968. Their protest struck deeper than the gun-blazing revolution of Che Guevara, than the violence and the slogans of *les événements* in Paris, the shouting and the hatred of the anti-Vietnam marches across London. This was a moment of great symbolic power; the fact that it happened in the theatrical context of a sporting arena greatly added to its potency. That something serious and important could arise from the glorious trivialities of sport was something that struck me with immense power.

And me, I marched deeper into the 60s, deeper into my own life, aware of the courage it takes to express "reservations", and of the price that must be paid for doing so. I learned that my heroes were not everyone's heroes. I was on Smith's side: and I hoped that if ever I had the opportunity to do so, I would have the courage to raise my own white fist with his.

1970s

11. Olga Korbut

COURAGE IS PART OF SPORT. Courage is also the most obvious part of the narrower view of heroism. Whoever heard of a hero who wasn't brave? (Actually, there have been many, and by no means all of them modern anti-heroes. Odysseus's response to his call-up for the Trojan War was to try and weasel out of it by pretending he was mad. Heroism has always been a complex subject.)

Courage has always been revered and admired. But it has generally been seen as a particularly male thing. Traditionally, we see courage as something to do with the Victoria Cross, with rescuing damsels from dragons, with Horatio holding the bridge, with the performance of very special and often rather bloody deeds at great personal risk. But this is a view that recognises only one aspect of courage, and a pretty specialised one.

Courage is not actually a rare thing at all. Like kindness, courage is something we run into every day. It is something we are all capable of, something we probably demonstrate ourselves on a regular enough basis. Courage can be practised in small, almost insignificant ways. It is a high moral virtue: but like all high moral virtues, it is within reach of us all. We recognise courage at its loftiest level because we know something about it from our own experience, as beneficiaries or even as the agents of courage. Everyone who has known fear understands courage, and everyone who has known fear cannot help but respond to spectacular acts of courage in another.

All sports require some kind of courage even to take part. For a start, you might get beaten. Worse, you might win: both possibilities require a modicum of courage. Many sports demand physical courage as a basic requirement for entry. Even on the village green, the cricket ball is hard and it hurts when it hits. Even a duffers' football match brings bruises. A fall from a slow horse hurts as much as a fall from a fast one.

Courage – in sport or anywhere else – is not confined to confrontation. Nor is physical strength necessary. Courage is protean, coming in a thousand shifting and changing forms. Those who see sporting courage only in heavyweight boxers tell us about nothing except their own limitations. And it was courage that thrilled me when I first set eyes on Olga Korbut.

She wasn't the best gymnast at the Munich Olympic Games of 1972. Ludmilla Tourisheva, who won the all-round individual gold medal, was better. But Korbut was the one who demanded the attention, and she did it with a combination of sizzling charisma and jaw-dropping bravery. She pulled off stunts that had never been tried before. The most spectacular was her back tuck somersault on the beam. I remember my disbelief as she landed thunderously, squarely and rock-solidly on the four-inch-wide beam. She seemed to slam her feet down with mad defiance: the emphasis with which she landed was a kind of up-yours to gravity. The second big trick took place on the asymmetric bars: she stood on the top of the higher bar while simultaneously clasping it with her hands. Then she sprang back, performed a backflip and caught the same bar on the way down.

That a human being could perform such a thing was a revelation. That a small girl could demonstrate such extraordinary courage forced me to rethink all kinds of traditional notions. And Korbut did it all with such style. Many, many other gymnasts have played the pixie since then, sexually ambiguous in lip-gloss and mascara and pre-pubescent bodies. Many of these have mugged at the cameras and flirted desperately with the judges.

Some have been fine gymnasts, one or two have been brilliant. But Korbut was not only the first of the elves: she was unique. She had an extraordinary look-at-me quality that was simultaneously innocent and knowing. At the Olympic Games, she won gold medals on the beam and on the floor; she ended her floor exercise with an outrageous flick of the wrist, a cock of the chin and a conspiratorial smirk: all of it redeemed from tackiness by her incandescent enjoyment of performance.

I missed the Munich Olympics because I was involved in mad travels around Europe at the time, trying to be the hero of my own story, despite my fears. I came back to tales of this Russian star, a girl from deep inside the Cold War who had enchanted the entire world. And when I saw her routines, I was lost in wonder.

It wasn't a sexual thing. Korbut was not desirable. Tourisheva was desirable all right: beautiful and though only two years older than Korbut, she was a woman while Korbut was a child. The fact that Korbut had a child's body didn't make me wonder about sexual ambiguities. It was the ambiguities of courage that disturbed me: the enthralling fact that courage could exist in such a physical form.

Gymnastics changed with Korbut, and not necessarily for the better. For years after that, the sport was dominated by tiny breast-less children performing ever-more devastating feats of agility. Gymnastics adjusted its parameters in the hope of finding another Olga, but to no avail. Korbut was unique. But a gymnast cannot be a star for ever.

It is not a problem many of us face: to fulfil your life, your destiny, your purpose, at the age of 17. You must live your adult life in the shadow of the great things you achieved as a child. Korbut was never as good again. She picked up two golds at the World Championships of 1974, and one more in the team event at the Olympic Games of 1976 in Montreal. She also won silver on the beam. But she found herself yesterday's star. Nadia Comaneci of Romania hit perfection and gave the world a string of perfect 10s.

Korbut's life after gymnastics has been complex and troubled; two divorces, a move to the United States, a prosecution for shoplifting: sad things for someone who was, though briefly, so greatly loved by so many people.

There are some people whose greatest joy in life is to perform. Anthony Powell wrote: "To exhibit themselves, perform before a crowd, is the keenest pleasure many people know, yet self-presentation without a basis in art is liable to crumble into dust and ashes." Many sporting performers love the public nature of what they do: but sporting ability, by its nature, is particularly suitable for crumbling. All the same, those who love performance would probably agree that the price is worth paying, that to have been brilliant once, briefly, and very young is still better than never having done it at all, despite the toll such achievements extract from later life.

12. Jan Tomaszewski

SPORT IS CONFRONTATIONAL and oppositional. Sport is about partisanship, especially when it's football. Sport constantly retells the most ancient of narratives: goodguys against bad guys. Our lot against your lot. As a result, we are inclined to impute to our lot a moral worth they don't necessarily deserve: and to confer a level of villainy on the opposition that has little basis in objective fact. There is a sense in which sport legitimises hatred. It's no longer acceptable for white people to hate black people, or for Christians to hate Jews. But it is considered OK for everyone who is not a Manchester United supporter to hate Manchester United, to hate all the Manchester United players, and especially, to hate the Manchester United manager. It is considered OK for English football followers to hate Germany, or at least, the German football team.

In some ways these hatreds are in inverted commas, cod hatreds, the best of their existence deriving from a form of ancient, time-honoured banter. But there are also times when the hatred – spurious, ridiculous, absurd – is frighteningly real. When England played Turkey in Sunderland in 2003, I walked among crowds of people who were all singing – loudly, unrestrainedly, unrebuked – "I'd rather be a Paki than a Turk". I remember another occasion, at the European Championship of 1996, when I was covering a Scotland game and got caught – jammed solid – in a crowd that wiled away the impasse by singing "If you all hate the English clap your hands". As I have never tired of pointing out, I got away with nothing more serious than sore palms.

In 1966, England won the World Cup. In 1970, an even better England team was knocked out in the quarter-finals by West Germany in an extraordinary match. We had been getting used to thinking of England as Brazil's great rival: the twin giants of the footballing world. We didn't know that the Germans would take on this role instead. Rather, we saw the famous picture of Pele and Bobby Moore exchanging shirts, and thought that here, encapsulated in this one image, was a rivalry that would enrich us all for years. From now on, every World Cup would ultimately be about England and Brazil.

England had hiccuped in the course of the qualifying tournament for the 1974 World Cup finals. This was irritating, but we all know that these things happen. We knew that England would put it right in the end, because England were, after all, Europe's Brazil. And even when England needed to win their last match, everyone knew they would do it. It might be an anxious evening, but England would get the win they needed. They had just beaten Austria 7-0 at Wembley; Poland would not get in their way for long.

That's not how it worked out. The reason for this was the Poland goalkeeper, Jan Tomaszewski. It was for him the game of a lifetime. He saved everything. He could do no wrong: or if he did, something or someone came to his rescue. It looked uncannily as if it was all preordained. England were all over Poland, chance after chance after chance. And Tomaszewski threw himself at everything with glorious, gaudy defiance. Poland scored a breakaway goal after a terrible bish from Norman Hunter; England equalised with a penalty from Allan Clarke. But England needed to win.

Time after time on that terrible night, I thought – I knew – that this was the one, this was the moment when the match would turn and from then on, everything would be all right.

And there was Tomaszewski. Again. And again. Parrying, punching, blocking. One save, from a Clarke volley, was startling. It was an utterly one-sided game, but England couldn't win it, and all because of Tomaszewski.

I remember the utter disbelief as the whistle blew. Life wasn't supposed to be like this. It was beyond comprehension. Beyond belief. England wouldn't be at the World Cup finals. England had failed. England were revealed before the world as they really were: second-raters. Afterwards, Brian Clough called Tomaszewski a clown, a fine example of vision blurred by partisanship.

I missed that. With the final whistle ringing in my ears, I was putting on my coat and marching up Rinsey Lane in Cornwall, heading for the Lion and Lamb, for I was taking a few days off from job-hunting at a borrowed cottage in Cornwall. I needed the air as much as the beer. But all the time, I was still thinking: what a game. What a game that keeper had. How glorious: to defy the team that thought they had a right to be considered the world's best. To destroy them.

I always saw myself as a goalkeeper. At that stage, I had played very little formal football, but in playgrounds, on the common, at five-a-side in the gym, I had always loved the diving about, the shot-stopping, the defiance. Tomaszewski's defiance was my defiance. A secret part of me loved the fact that my own team had been defied by the inspiration of a single individual.

Losing to Poland was not the terrible disgrace we all thought at the time. Poland were a very good team: they went on to finish third in the World Cup finals, beating Argentina, Italy and Brazil on the way. Tomaszewski saved two penalties in the course of the tournament, the first time a goalkeeper had done so.

Tomaszewski remembers that night not as the best, but as the luckiest performance of his life. He remembers a moment, right in the early minutes of the game, when he was playing about with the ball in his penalty area. Clarke plunged in on the ball, and caught Tomaszewski on the hand, a painful injury that required prolonged treatment after the match. Clarke was a touch away from scoring. "I was so frightened I didn't see him," Tomaszewski said. Before the match, he had been praying that Poland wouldn't lose by seven goals. When England strolled out, they looked, he said, "like they were already leading 3-0". Tomaszewski put this fear to good use: alchemised it into inspiration as great players do. Well, Tomaszewski was short of greatness if you bring in such factors as long-term consistency, but that night, he was indisputably great.

The stresses of partisanship can do odd things to the mind, and frequently one of the odder effects is to bring out not only a reluctant admiration for your team's rivals, but a strange sort of love. Tomaszewski became a glorious emblem of defiance: and those of us who were shouting for England savour his glory entirely by means of pain. Tomaszewski inflicted great pain on us; how can we fail to find a little love for him? How can we fail to accord him the status of hero?

13. Johan Cruyff

PELE WAS PROBABLY A better footballer than Johan Cruyff, but he hasn't made this panheroikon. This is not because Pele wasn't great: it's because he was never one of my heroes. There was never a time when he had power over my imagination. I watched him during the World Cup of 1966, but in that tournament, he was brutally kicked out of it and was unable to show us his best. Four years later, at the World Cup of 1970, he had what was probably his greatest tournament. No doubt he'd have been a hero for me had I watched, but I didn't see a ball kicked. I was travelling haphazardly around Greece at the time, a three-month teenage adventure that absorbed me utterly. I was scarcely aware that a World Cup was going on. Pele passed me by. And if that was my loss, it was one I made good four years later.

It was 1974 and I had just got my first proper job. I was to start as a cub reporter for the *Surrey Mirror* in Redhill the day after the World Cup final. During my last few weeks of freedom, I made a series of visits to neighbours, old family friends, who lived a short way from me in Bristol. Their son Jeremy, then about 14, and I would watch the World Cup, for I had no television in my basement flat in a crumbling Clifton crescent. It was with Jeremy that I saw Holland; I saw Cruyff; I saw greatness.

It wasn't just Cruyff, of course. It was that marvellous thought, that marvellous phrase. *Total football.* Total football was the ultimate expression of the game: a concept of dizzying brilliance made possible by the genius of a single man.

The theory of total football was that no player had a fixed position, right-back, centre-half, left wing. You just had footballers, ten renaissance men, each one thinking both creatively and responsibly. In practice it wasn't quite so perfect; there were players in the Dutch team who were clearly defenders and not much else, and wingers who were better on the peripheries. But the idea's the thing, and I was in love with the idea.

I was to work in the newsroom at the *Surrey Mirror,* covering magistrates' court, police calls, residents' rows, car crashes, all that sort of thing. I had no thought whatsoever of working in sport. I thought that working in sport was for arseholes, for people far more trivial than myself. Sport was not something I gave serious thought to. Later on, giving serious thought to the trivialities of sport became the way I made my living: funny how things turn out. And so, maybe 20 years after I had watched the World Cup with Jeremy, I came up with my theory of footballing greatness. The thing that distinguishes a great footballer from a very, very good one is leadership. Not leadership of the follow-me-lads kind: rather, in every truly great player you find an ability to create a team around himself, one in which every member is somehow forced to play beyond his normal ability. Pele had that, so did Diego Maradona and Zinedine Zidane. George Best didn't; Bobby Charlton didn't.

But Cruyff had it and – though we will come to him in a few moments – so too did Franz Beckenbauer. And Cruyff expressed this gift more vividly than most, because of the gorgeous, brilliant, intoxicating way his team played. One of the things that appealed to me about Cruyff and about total football was the fact that Cruyff played like an intellectual. Cruyff's football seemed to be moved by ideas and concepts rather than circumstances and confrontations.

Cruyff always seemed detached: set apart from the others, slightly remote from the hurly-burly of international football. He was aware of the difference between himself and the rest, aware of his uniqueness, yet he never forgot that he needed the others to complete his work. This was not exactly modesty. Rather, he made the team an extension of his nature: an expression of his will. His team was his masterpiece.

In theory, Cruyff was the centre-forward of that Holland team. But this was total football. So he would play for a while as a winger and send in swirling, laser-guided crosses. When marked man to man, he would sometimes drop back and play as centre-half for a spell: what was the poor marker supposed to do then? But Cruyff's real position was conductor. As in orchestra. He had wonderful acceleration, or seemed to; he always said that in fact, he wasn't terribly quick. It was his mind that was fast, his timing that allowed him to burst through defences as if fired from a gun. The truth revealed here is that Cruyff prided himself more on his mental than his physical gifts.

The Holland team filled me with an incredulous joy. They beat Uruguay 2-0 in their opener, took an easy against Sweden with a goalless draw, then massacred Bulgaria 4-1. The tournament then went into a second group stage: Holland beat Argentina 4-0, East Germany 2-0 and finally Brazil 2-0. They were unstoppable. In the main, Cruyff was flamboyant only in the devastation he wreaked on the opposition, unlike say, Best, who was flamboyant every time he touched the ball. Pele and Maradona always sought the spectacular. But Cruyff had that touch of detachment that made him a different player to watch. There was one exception to this rule: the Cruyff Turn. This was a move, now found in all the coaching manuals, in which a player fakes one way and then makes a 180-degree turn. It is the ultimately humiliating trick: to have your would-be tackler running as hard as he can in the wrong direction.

The second group stage led straight to the final, where Holland met West Germany, ancestral enemies of the Dutch, the Dutch forever one-down against them. And the West Germans were led by Beckenbauer, who had invented the role of the attacking sweeper. It all went wrong for the Dutch straight from the kick-off. It went wrong because they took the lead. Cruyff it was who kicked off: and 13 passes later, he was felled in the box by Uli Hoeness. Johan Neeskens crashed the penalty home. The Dutch were 1-0 up almost before the game had begun. After that, for 25 minutes they danced rings of airy brilliance around the Germans: dominating, teasing, tormenting, revelling in their brilliance, in their superiority. They did so without scoring. The Germans won 2-1.

Heroes are not always winners, not even in sport. Instead, we must sometimes look for glory in failure. Did the desire to taunt rather than destroy the ancient enemy come from Cruyff? Was he a willing part of it? Certainly, he held his sport's ultimate prize in his hands, and let it slip. Heroes are not supposed to be perfect human beings: sporting heroes are not supposed to be perfect at sport.

Cruyff had a long and distinguished club career, with Ajax and Barcelona, and then a long and mostly successful period in management. He didn't play in the World Cup of 1978: it was widely thought that he was having one of his rows and throwing a sulk; later he explained that his family has been going through the horror of a kidnapping scare.

Cruyff was at his best in 1974, and that Holland team was the perfect embodiment of his genius. I was in love with the intellectual arrogance of the performance. In love, too, with its ultimate failure. And anyway – is it really such a failure, to create a masterpiece? The shelves around me in my study as I write these words are groaning beneath the weight of flawed masterpieces. Cruyff's World Cup was a flawed masterpiece: an intellectually brilliant concept that was both flawed and made great by its human realities.

14. Muhammad Ali

I NEVER CARED FOR CASSIUS CLAY. I never much cared for Muhammad Ali, either. All that showing off and shouting. It wasn't that I found this behaviour inappropriate in a black man. I thought it was inappropriate in anyone. We didn't get him, at my school. There were a lot of other things we didn't get either.

But when Clay, when Ali began, it was still the 60s. We were all of us caught between the ideas of our parents, our schoolteachers, and those around us – the Establishment, as it was then called – and the realisation that these ideas were not fixed, immutable and settled for all time. We could make up our own minds, if we wanted to. We could even try and think for ourselves. But at first, we were repelled by Clay because he affronted our parents. We disliked him because we were supposed to dislike him.

Cassius Clay changed his name to Muhammad Ali in 1964, after he beat Sonny Liston to become the heavyweight champion of the world. We all thought this was a bit silly. A gimmick, like Richard Starkey becoming Ringo Starr. There is always something slightly odd about name-changers. It is too naked an attempt to become somebody else. We didn't get Ali's contention that Cassius Clay was a slave name. We didn't understand the social issues behind all this. How could we? We had prep to do. There was scarcely a non-white person in the school: how could we know about social injustice? We were too busy perpetrating it.

The 60s polarised people, as I have said, and Vietnam was one of the things that divided us. If Vietnam goes, then all of Asia goes. Goes where? And when Asia's gone, it'll be Australia next, is that what you want? And after that... I was beginning to hold other views, but I still felt no special admiration, still less love, for Ali. I know, I know: everybody who was brought up in the 60s loved Muhammad Ali and was opposed to the Vietnam War. Most people came to this realisation round about 1976.

Ali refused to be drafted, and as a result, he was suspended from boxing for three and half years. This gesture divided us still more. He was a hero, he was a coward, he was making a social protest, he just didn't want to go and fight. The glorious simplicity of his stance – "I ain't got nothing against them Vietcong" – somehow passed us by. And though by then I was espousing all kinds of revolutionary notions, still Ali meant little. He seemed a curiously trivial figure. Like John Lennon, but without the songs.

In the years that followed, long after he had retired, long after his physical deterioration set in, Ali only ever had one answer to the most-often-asked question: "How do you wish to be remembered?" "As the greatest fighter of all time." His sport was central to his life, to the way he understood himself: and yet he gave up three and half years of it on a point of principle. Ali never believed that his story was about social significance. He was a fighter who got caught up in turbulent times: but it was the fighting that mattered.

But I was cut off even from this. Boxing has never touched me. Ali is the only boxer in this panheroikon. When I became a sportswriter, I started writing against boxing right from the beginning. Boxing is not a sport – that is to say a metaphor – but a duel. You can get injured and for that matter, concussed in other sports, and I have suffered some grievous blows myself, but these things happen when something has gone badly wrong. When someone gets seriously injured in boxing, it is because something has gone horribly right.

Where was I on October 30, 1974? I had by then been working for the *Surrey Mirror* for three months. I was still living in a shared house at the end of the runway at Gatwick Airport. Perhaps I watched it on the television in the shared sitting room. Perhaps it was a rerun. But anyway, I watched, and was astounded, and I realised then that no matter what else was true about Ali, and never mind what was obviously true about boxing, I was unquestionably watching the greatest fighter that ever lived.

Ali's comeback after his suspension had involved such unthinkable setbacks as defeat. He eventually beat those who had beaten him, but by this time, boxing was dominated by George Foreman. The terrifying George Foreman, with the most explosive punch that had ever been seen in a ring. He would destroy Ali, that much was clear. Ali, aged 32, was going to destroy himself merely by entering the ring.

He did.

He also won, of course. After the first round, in which he confused Foreman by attacking with a right-hand lead, he then switched tactics. The fight was in Kinshasa, in what was then Zaire, now the Democratic Republic of the Congo (name changes again). It was cruelly hot. And Ali lay back on the ropes, and allowed Foreman to attack. Mostly, Foreman missed, or saw his blows deflected. Certainly, he never landed a knock-out blow. But Ali took punches aplenty. It looked like suicide. Foreman poured out all his strength in this wild attempt to put Ali down. And then Ali uncoiled himself from the ropes and took Foreman out with a neat combination in the eighth.

The monster had been slain. Ali's tactical brilliance and his wild courage in adopting so unconventional a tactic showed his genius for boxing. And it was in that extraordinary victory that I understood not only his sporting brilliance, but the meaning of his career as a rebel. In that unique detonation of magnificence, I could see what he had sacrificed: three and half years of his peak. And yet for all that he prided himself – above everything else – on his sporting achievement, it was a sacrifice that could not be ducked.

I have subsequently attended Ali love-fests in the United States: ghastly occasions when Ali, shuffling, shambling and slurring words, with the ghost of the ancient devil faintly discernible in a minute twitch of the lips, the faintest narrowing of an eye, is cheered to the echo: the greatest, the greatest that ever was. Here is a man who craves love: here is a man who deliberately became a hate object. He divided America as well as my school: he divided the world as well as America. He did that by telling us, in deeds far more than in words – though he was, in his way, a master of them – that a black man was as good as a white man any day, if not a damn sight better. For that, he was hated. For that, he is now loved. And always I wonder: were his injuries, his terrible deterioration, the prerequisite for this love? Did the world need to see him more or less castrated before love became unconditional?

The Rumble in the Jungle was the greatest hour of The Greatest. It was also the beginning of the end. After that, Ali relied less and less on his speed – how could he, in his thirties? – and more and more on his ability to take a punch. In the end, his determination to carry on, his love for combat, his pursuit of his own brilliance – a pursuit given sharpness by those lost years – saw him acquire the subtle and cumulative injuries that led to his physical decline. Ali was a fighter who became a roaring apostle of peace; he became a fighter again when some kind of peace was achieved; and when his fighting days were done, became a shuffling, smiling, sweet-natured apostle for universal love. But he still wants us to remember him as a fighter.

15. Colin Cowdrey

M.J.K. Smith captained Warwickshire and England in the 60s. He disappointed as much as he thrilled, often failing to find form when it really mattered.

Anita Lonsbrough worked as a clerk in Huddersfield Town Hall – and she beat the best of the best in the 1960 Rome Olympics in the 200m breaststroke.

Don Thompson, sporting his homemade sun hat, arrives at Rome's Stadio Olimpico en route to winning the 50 km walk.

Abebe Bikila running barefoot down the Appian Way in 1960 – faster and better than everyone who took shoes for granted.

Bobby Charlton unleashes hope as he scores a glorious goal against Mexico in the second round of the 1966 World Cup.

George Best in
action in 1966: a
master of excess.

Vibart takes a kick backwards at the fence - his risky signature move.

Left: Garry Sobers, a truly brilliant all-rounder. Not only talented on the cricket pitch, he also played golf, basketball and football for Barbados.

Right: Tommie Smith, centre, raising his gloved fist in support of the American civil rights movement at the 1968 Olympics. He lost his gold medal as a result but later–much later–he was accepted as an American hero.

Bob Beamon leaps to victory. He achieved greatness in just one jump.

Olga Korbut at the 1972 Olympics in Munich awed the crowds with her courageous display on the uneven bars.

Jan Tomaszewski saves yet another goal in the 1974 World Cup match between Poland and England. He was single-handedly responsible for ending the hopes of the English.

Johan Cruyff was the master of "total football" for the Dutch team at the 1974 World Cup. He also showcased his new invention the "Cruyff Turn".

An unmistakeable figure. Muhammad Ali sacrificed the peak of his career for his beliefs and fought as a rebel both in and out of the ring.

Above: Colin Cowdrey
batting in 1975. A hugely
generous man, Cowdrey was
the first of my heroes I met
face to face.

Right: Arthur Ashe
celebrates his win over
Jimmy Conners in the
Wimbledon final of 1975.

Right: Out of the ordinary
came the extraordinary.
Steele quietly and
forgettably gets on with
despatching the attack of
Lillie and Thomson in the
summer of 1976.

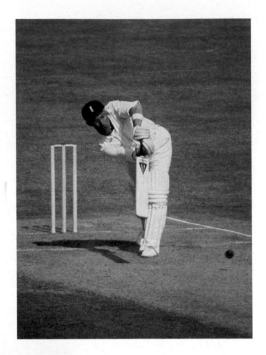

Left: The famous victory
celebration of Bjorn Borg,
this time beating McEnroe
to win the Wimbledon
title in 1980.

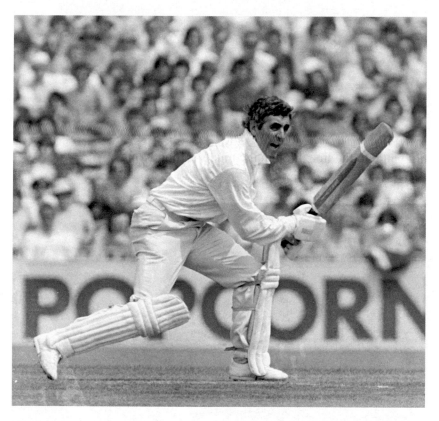

Mike Brearley playing against New Zealand in 1979. He was better at the thinking than the smiting side of the game.

Fiji battle to the line through the mud in Hong Kong.

Shergar's truly remarkable win at the 1981 Derby. He more or less hacked up with the widest winning margin in the history of the race.

Left: Ian Botham.
Captained England to eight
draws, four defeats and
zero wins and yet was man
of the series against
Australia in 1981.

Right: Torvill and
Dean performing the
unforgettable *Bolero*
at the 1984 Olympics.

The great master of fear, Malcolm Marshall, in action.

A young Martina
Navratilova playing at
Wimbledon in the 80s.

PERHAPS HEROISM IS AT its best when it is futile. Perhaps heroism is at its best when a person is brave, when a person makes sacrifices, when a person is prepared to give everything – and all to no avail. All in order, if you like, to lose with beauty. Heroism is perhaps at its finest when there's nothing in it for the hero: only pain, humiliation and defeat. But the hero prefers to embrace such things, rather than to take any of the easy options.

Colin Cowdrey was a youth garlanded with all the talents, a games player of extraordinary gifts. I had watched him throughout the 60s; he played cricket for England with M.J.K. Smith, and swapped bouts of captaincy with him. Cowdrey captained England 27 times, in three different spells, without ever once looking like a natural leader of men. He was the first man to play 100 Tests.

He was round in the face, and always on the stout side for a professional sportsman. But he also had the fat man's incongruous grace. He was a naturally diffident man: easy-going, eager to be liked, but he also had a very pronounced and old-fashioned sense of duty. He didn't relish confrontation, but if it was his duty to face up to an opponent, especially in difficult and demanding circumstances, Cowdrey wouldn't think of stepping back. That would be selfish. His best innings was probably the century he made against Australia when he played Ray Lindwall and Keith Miller, two of the fastest bowlers that ever lived, on a bad pitch. He also, with a mixture of talent and cunning, batted the brilliant West Indian spinner Sonny Ramadhin into ordinariness.

But even so, he was no hero of mine. I was for M.J.K.: and though I admired Cowdrey very much, there was no vacancy for him in my panheroikon. Then, three and half years after he had played what seemed to be his last Test match, he became a hero for me.

It was the Ashes winter of 1974–75. I was working in Redhill. The cricket came to us in newsreel highlights, and in reports in newspapers. And they told us of two ferocious Australian fast bowlers: Dennis Lillee and Jeff Thomson. They were fast, yes. But they also bowled bouncers. Not as a startle tactic, but as a matter of routine. England batsmen were to be dominated, frightened, hurt. In those days, they played without helmets, without the body armour that became standard. Just a pad and, especially, a box.

Odd to think that England went into the series in the belief that Australia didn't have much in the locker when it came to fast bowling. But the emergence of Lillee and Thomson, and their ferocious assault on body and mind, changed everything – changed cricket for ever, if it came to that. It was a new and ferocious world. Thomson said ridiculous things like "the sound of breaking Pommy skulls is music to my ears". And in the first Test match, England lost two front-line batsmen; Dennis Amiss and John Edrich both had broken hands. What to do?

Send for Cowdrey. That was the almost absurd response. Send for Cowdrey, who was aged 42 and hadn't played Test cricket for three and a half years. Send him across the world, and put him into the second Test at Perth after three days of preparation. And Cowdrey went. He came onto the pitch, and at once spoke to Thomson. "I don't believe we've met. My name's Cowdrey."

Cowdrey was more portly than ever, stately in his bearing.

He came out like a throwback, like a lost knight brought out from the deep past to settle the ills of the modern world. And of course, he failed, but there was glory in his failure. I remember the rather mannered, faintly insolent off-stump leave-shot that he played disdainfully to both Lillee and Thomson, and one astonishingly late offside dab.

But I remember most the incongruous sight of this patrician old buffer at the crease as the wild young colonial bowlers brought in the modern world and sent it humming around his head. Cowdrey made 22 and 41 as England lost: it was to be the high point of his series. As Lillee and Thomson prospered, and Thomson took 33 wickets, Cowdrey ended up with a series average of 18.33.

A year or so later, I met him. Cowdrey was always a generous man, with exquisite manners and, of course, a fine sense of duty. So, out of either kindness or duty, he agreed to the impertinent request of a cub reporter from his local paper, for I had learned that he lived right out on the fringe of the *Surrey Mirror*'s circulation area. So I went to visit him, to do an interview for the weekly "Profile" slot. It was, I think, the first time I had met a famous person in the line of duty, the first time I had had dealings with a top-class professional athlete.

We ran short of time because the photographer was having problems. Cowdrey had to drive to Canterbury, and invited me to join him. We continued the conversation in the car. Eventually, after an hour or so of talk, he dropped me at the train station and I made my way back to Redhill. Quite thrilled by what I had been doing. Utterly taken with the generosity of the man.

The one question I had wanted to ask him was one that I

now know was absurd, naïve, ridiculous. It was this: "Why did you go to Australia? Why did you want to go and play against Lillee and Thomson?" There was a sense in which Cowdrey was almost consciously dismantling his own legend, deliberately besmirching his own record. He was changing the symbolic weight of his own story, a story that mattered to every one who had followed the English cricket team at the time when he was at his best. No one wanted to see this great cricketer fail. No one wanted to see this great cricketer look like an ordinary cricketer. No one wanted to spoil the Cowdrey myth.

And of course, Cowdrey never gave such things a moment's thought. "I just wanted to go out and see if I could do it." Athletes are very seldom interested in the past. Come to that, they are not much interested in the future. It is the present that absorbs them: perhaps this rare talent for living in the moment is a defining trait of great athletes. Perhaps of heroes, who knows? For such people, records don't matter: the way people turn your story into legend doesn't matter: your own myth doesn't matter at all. Doing it is what absorbs you. Winning, yes, not losing, if at all possible, but above all, being there.

When I became a sportswriter for *The Times*, I would bump into Cowdrey from time to time. It was always a delight to see him. He had the generous person's knack of always being pleased to see you. He was always agreeable, always good company, a great giggler. I remember being stranded with him in an airport lounge in, I think, Calcutta. It was two in the morning, planes delayed for at least another three hours, maybe four. We settled into chairs in various states of resignation and despair. And then, after an hour or so, a miracle took place. A man entered, soft-footed and pushing a cart full of glorious booze. Almost at once I found myself clutching a perfectly enormous whisky. Cowdrey awoke from his own coma, took his own drink, and we fell into a hilarious bantering conversation that lifted our spirits and bore us in due course to the plane in great good heart. Cricket and booze and companionship: fine things.

While we were in that car on the way to Canterbury, I asked Cowdrey for the secret of success in sport. Not a very good question, I admit. But Cowdrey had a very good answer: "You must be perpetually two years old," he said. Then, life can be reduced to the passage of ball from hand to bat to boundary: it is not just the most important but the only thing in the world. And so life in the now becomes the only conceivable reality. Perhaps all sporting heroes – perhaps all heroes of every kind – need at least in some part of themselves to be perpetually two years old. Perhaps we all do.

16. Arthur Ashe

SOMETIMES HEROES ARE DEFINED by those they oppose. St George needed the dragon to make his heroic nature clear to the world. Arthur Ashe needed Jimmy Connors. The two of them made a classic opposed pair: a perfect heroic antithesis. One was tall, dignified, rather patrician in nature, with a college degree. He had been an officer in the army, he was long on loyalty, being a great supporter of the Davis Cup and of the men's tennis tour. His style was elegant, a little cerebral, with something of an air of detachment.

The other was a scrapper with filthy manners, a grown man full of urchin defiance, a great giver of the finger, a great grabber of his crotch, a person who thought it amusing to place his racket-handle between his legs and toy with it. Foul-mouthed, abusive, flagrantly loyal only to himself, he revelled in his own obnoxious qualities, and of these, there were many.

This perfect opposition was doubled in force by the fact that Ashe was a black man who had achieved everything from nothing, while Connors was a white middle-class kid. Ashe had to leave Richmond, Virginia because the place was segregated. No white kids would – or for that matter could – play against Ashe, because he was black. His family moved to St Louis, so that he could get decent opposition. He went to the University of California in Los Angeles, became a second lieutenant in the US Army, went back to tennis and became the first black player to represent the United States in the Davis Cup.

Connors, nine years younger, was, it must be said, a much better player. As Ashe was moving into the later stages of his career, Connors was tearing up trees with his aggressive baseline style, which came from his brilliance at taking the ball on the rise. "I hate tennis balls, I want to hit them so hard they never come back," Connors once said. This was his game plan, his mission statement, his life. Connors was mad about money, and mad, too, about getting one up on everybody else. He loved playing in lucrative exhibitions, never mind the men's tour. He was involved in World Team Tennis, in direct opposition to the Association of Tennis Professionals, the main men's tour. As a result of all this, Connors was barred from the French Open in 1974, and was sued by the ATP. The president of the ATP was Ashe.

The Wimbledon crowd was always in two minds about Connors. His thrilling shot-making was loudly cheered, but there were embarrassed silences at the pelvic thrusts with which he celebrated big points. Ashe was always something of a Wimbledon favourite. So when the two of them met in the Wimbledon final of 1975, Ashe was the one who got the cheers. Doubly so, because he was an underdog. A gracious, graceful underdog lined up against a charmless up-yours cad with a fascination for his own crotch: it was natural that Ashe was cheered.

The only problem was that Ashe was certain to lose. Bookies had Connors at 10-1 on. He was at the peak of his powers: John McEnroe and Bjorn Borg had yet to launch their challenges for greatness. It was Connors's world. Not everybody was happy about that, but Ashe seemed too frail a weapon, too decent a man, to stand up against this ferocious gobbing competitor who wielded his racket like an axe-murderer. Connors was a youth; Ashe was nearly 32.

Ashe worked out his strategy over dinner the night before.

He wrote down five or six points on a piece of paper, and the following day, he looked at it during the changeovers. In normal circumstances, Ashe was a frank striker of the ball: serve big, hit deep, volley sharp and crisp. That was the standard package in men's tennis back then. Connors, with all his power from the back-court and his double-fister, was playing the modern game before modern racket technology made it easy. He really was a phenomenally talented player; Ashe realised that to go out there and try and out-hit was to give the match away.

So Ashe gave him junk. Changes of pace, spin, drop-shots, lobs. Connors habitually devoured pace like a shark in a feeding frenzy: so Ashe gave him no pace. He offered a sliced serve wide to the famous double-fister: without pace, Connors had to generate his own, and that wasn't his game. Connors was out-played, outfoxed. Ashe reeled off the first two sets 6-1, 6-1.

Throughout his career, the one thing that could make you love Connors was the fact that he never gave up. I once saw him two sets down to Patrick McEnroe in the US Open. It was a night match, it had gone eleven o'clock. When Connors was broken in the third set, everyone in the expensive seats gave up on him. There was a silent, hanging pause, and then an invasion: everyone from high up in the stands came marauding down to the expensive and abandoned places: "We're still here, Jimmy!" shouted someone. Connors heard. It had become his kind of occasion. I was still there myself when, some time after one in the morning, Connors won in five sets. He was magnificent.

So of course Connors came back against Ashe, swearing

and blasting, and took the third 7-5, working himself up into one of his frenzies. It looked like a momentum shift, of the kind I was to see years later when he played against McEnroe. But here was the most beautiful part of the match: Connors, working himself up, all fist-pumping and muttering and glaring, and at the changeovers, Ashe doing the precise opposite. He withdrew. He closed his eyes and absented himself. He sat comfortably – this was the first year that the players could sit down during the changeovers at Wimbledon – and went into a brief, meditative trance, his Afro standing out around his head like a halo. He was a man from another world, come to rescue us from all the distasteful things of modern life.

Ashe considered a change of plan: surprising Connors by going into the fourth set swinging. But he decided to stick to his game plan. He found himself 3-0 down: but still he kept the faith. These were the defining few moments of his career. He won six of the next seven games and with them the match.

Ashe lived a life of almost sanctified respectability; not because he was ostentatiously virtuous, but because he was simply a good man, very serious about his responsibilities in such matters as race and tennis. He had a heart attack four years after he won Wimbledon, and had a quadruple bypass. In 1988, he became HIV positive after a blood transfusion, and so campaigned, with the dignity that was inseparable from him, for AIDS awareness. He died in 1993. The centre court at Flushing Meadow, where the US Open is held, is called the Arthur Ashe Stadium. There have been better American tennis players, but Ashe played the role of the symbolic black champion as well as such a difficult and awkward role could possibly be played.

And me, I loved the cerebral nature of his victory, the meditation, the way he undid an opponent whose defeat was so sweet to watch.

17. David Steele

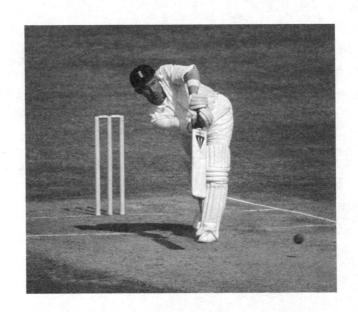

HERE IS ANOTHER HERO who defied the greatest fast bowlers of his time, probably of all time. He stood firm against Dennis Lillee and Jeff Thomson – but you've heard about someone doing that before. However, the tale of David Steele is nothing like the Colin Cowdrey story. It could hardly be more different. It was a different kind of heroism: Steele was a different kind of hero altogether. Cowdrey was a great cricketer. He was already a great cricketer when he stepped out against Lillee and Thomson. He had been famous all his professional life. Cowdrey was greatly loved long before he went out to face Lillee and Thomson. It was his willingness to risk the fine things he had achieved – his reputation, his story, his myth – that made the last act of his cricketing story so fine.

But Steele's story is quite different. Only the opponents were the same. For a start, Steele succeeded where Cowdrey failed. But the crucial part of his story lies in his obscurity: his almost absurd unlikeliness: his staggeringly unheroic appearance.

England had been hammered in Australia, losing the Test series 4-1, despite Cowdrey's courage. Australia came to England in 1975, and England were promptly hammered again, losing the first match by an innings. Cowdrey was not asked to play: he had done his bit. There was a dreadful inevitability about the defeat. Everyone in the country felt defeated. It was a defeated sort of time: the air of England was rank with defeat. An apparently unending series of sporting defeats reflected the greater defeats of the wider world. The previous year had brought the three-day week, a drastic austerity measure introduced to save electricity.

Strikes, power cuts and shortages had become part of the routine of life. It seemed that we in England were no longer capable of resisting defeat. We had become compliant, part of the process. The England football team had failed to qualify for the 1974 World Cup finals, and were in the throes of messing up qualification for the 1976 European Championship. The England rugby team was hopeless, winning just one game in the 1975 Five Nations tournament. There was no one in any of the individual sports to inspire anybody in England: not even a Scotsman who could be called British. Well, there was the England cricket captain, Mike Denness, but he was not inspiring much confidence in anyone, not even the Scots.

England looked set for a summer-long humiliation against Australia. Denness resigned after the first Test. The selectors, at their wits' end, took a punt on the almost insanely optimistic Tony Greig. Greig was South African-born and sounded it in everything he said. England's weary acceptance of misery was anathema to him. He came into the job bubbling, like Michael Caine in *The Italian Job*, with a million great ideas. One of them, and it looked, in the face of considerable competition, like the daftest of them all, was to bring in a batsman from Northamptonshire: a cricketer who had never been anything special, even by the standards of Northamptonshire. He had scored 16 centuries in 12 seasons, with a career average of 31. In came Steele.

The second Test of the series was at Lord's. It was Steele's first appearance for England. He was 33 and looked ten years older. He had steel spectacles and steel-grey hair. He had never been in the home dressing room at Lord's. He was given the always-troubled position of number three, and was required to bat almost at once, as the first wicket fell at 10. At Lord's, a batsman must walk through the pavilion, through the crowds of MCC members and their guests, to make his way to the pitch: Steele, unfamiliar with the layout, went down one flight of stairs too many and found himself in the gents'. He just about managed to get onto the field before he could be timed out. Steele says that it is not, alas, true that Thomson greeted him with the words: "Who's this? Father bloody Christmas?"

But Lillee and Thomson went for him in a kind of feeding frenzy: and Steel stood firm. As he did so, he projected an extraordinary air of ordinariness: as if he simply couldn't see what all the fuss was about. He just pottered about his daily business, taking on two of the finest fast bowlers that had ever lived. This was the tone of the match, and of the summer. Steel made 50 and 45 at Lord's, and England got away with a draw. They also drew the other two matches in a series that was shortened to make room for the World Cup that followed. Steele averaged 60 in that series, but he didn't make a century. That would have been too flamboyant, altogether inappropriate. His post-Lord's scores were 73, 92, 39 and 66. England built their defiance around Steele, and Steele just quietly and unforgettably got on with it. Routinely top scorer in the England innings, he just stood there in his unassuming way and made damn sure that they did not pass.

England was overjoyed to have such a hero: a hero of his time if ever there was one: a grey man who stood firm in the face of trouble in a grey era. Inevitably, he was BBC Sports Personality for 1975, and if you look down the list across the years, you can find some great names alongside others voted in with bewildering capriciousness. Among them there are losers whose place in public affection seem baffling in retrospect: Damon Hill chosen for coming second in the Formula One World Drivers' Championship; Greg Rusedski for being runner-up in the US Open tennis tournament. But don't put Steele in that number. Sure, England didn't actually win. But there was no one else around who was winning anything. What Steele was doing was Not Losing. And that was as good as it was going to get, back then.

The following summer brough blazing heat, water shortages, and a wild boast from Greig that England would make West Indies grovel. By this time, the West Indies had themselves been battered by Lillee and Thomson, and their captain, Clive Lloyd, decided that if cricket was to be played like that, the West Indies could do the same, only better. So the West Indies lined up with four fearsome fast bowlers, not just two. Steele found himself batting against Andy Roberts, Michael Holding, Wayne Daniel and Vanburn Holder. He was as resolute as ever, scoring 106 – a century at last – as England resisted at Trent Bridge, and after two Tests, were still not losing. But the West Indies took the final three in an overwhelming outpouring of speed and anger and defiance. Steele had played eight Tests and faced some of the most formidable bowling in history. He was dropped for the winter tour of India, on the grounds that he was not a great player of spin bowling, India's traditional strength.

There was something appropriate in that. Steele was not needed when things got easier. He was only useful when things looked impossible.

Clive Taylor, writing in the *Sun*, hit on the phrase that is always associated with him: "The bank clerk that went to war". Cricket is not war, but when it is played with this level of intensity and violence, war is not an entirely unsuitable metaphor. Steele looked like a man unfamiliar with, perhaps even unaware of, his own courage: acting on the straightforward assumption that if there was no one else to do it, he had better get on with it. He was a hero who, it seems, had no prior intention of ever doing anything heroic, who only got an opportunity to have his heroic nature tested by chance and whim, and having been asked, diligently and apologetically played the hero for as long as it was necessary, and then returned to obscurity. Steele was a man who got lumbered with heroism: and being lumbered, bore the burden – well, heroically.

18. Bjorn Borg

THEY THOUGHT HE WAS cold. Unemotional. Uninvolved. A person who had a kind of freakish advantage because he was somehow immune to the agonies and ecstasies that normal human beings feel. Those people who thought such things must have been putting the kettle on when he won a championship point.

Because it was only when Bjorn Borg won a Wimbledon final that he allowed the world to see that it mattered. Then he would drop to his knees and clasp his head. *Time* magazine called him "The Incredible Tennis Machine" when they put him on the cover, for sheer reckless love of the cliché. But if so, he was William Burroughs's soft machine: a machine that bled and wept. He was tremendously talented at pretending to be the iceborg, at pretending to be a machine, relishing the fact that his apparent detachment broke the hearts of his opponents, but it was all just an act. During Wimbledon, it wasn't just that he didn't shave, so that he invariably walked into the final with half a beard. He didn't have sex either. He seemed to allow himself no emotion of any kind. But when at last he had the victory he craved, the ghost in the machine would walk.

Borg was not unemotional: rather, he was the master of his emotions. This mastery was an acquired skill, for he began his career as a tennis brat. "I swore, I threw rackets, I cheated." He was precociously talented – he played in the Davis Cup for Sweden when he was 15. In 1973, when he was 17, he played Wimbledon for the first time and reached the quarter-finals. The following year, he started to win the big prizes. He had learned the lesson learned by the schoolboys in Kipling's notorious *Stalky & Co*: "They had settled into their stride now. Their eyes ceased to sparkle; their faces were blank; their hands hung beside them without a twitch. They were learning, at the expense of a fellow-countryman, the lesson of their race, which is to put away all emotion and entrap the alien at the proper time."

There are many reasons for choosing a hero, but there are two principal ones. The first is because the person admired is like you; the second, because he is not like you. Many of us have a special admiration for traits we could not possess in a thousand years, seeing in the hero some kind of mystical completion of ourselves. (I will confess here a longing to be the Man with No Name, the Clint Eastwood hero of the Dollars Westerns.)

There is an equal and opposite tendency to make heroes of people who represent a kind of super-me: who have my own talents or my own nature magnified to a fantastic extent. James Joyce, the word-drunk lover of patterns and repetitions, attempting to turn a novel into both music and liturgy, represents the logical conclusion of a journey I can only tentatively begin.

In sport, and particularly in sport in the last half of the 1970s, Borg was both my antithesis and my apotheosis. He was the super-me: he was my precise opposite. Because he did indeed look a little like me: a long face, a wispy beard, hair to his shoulders. I had been known to wear a headband in my time. He was – or at least he looked like – a hippy taking the Establishment by means of the force of his unstoppable brilliance, and that was a role I naturally aspired to. I was by then beginning my life in the professional world, having left a hippified student life behind. So in a sense Borg was out there doing it for me: for all of us who swore we would never rejoin straight society. But that self-mastery that Borg came to: that was utterly alien to my nature. In truth, in terms of temperament, I had more in common with Borg's greatest opponent, John McEnroe: a thwarted artistry and a vile temper.

Borg won the French Open in 1974 and 1975, making it clear that he was a clay-court specialist, a pummeller, an exploiter of patience, an out-hitter, an out-laster. In 1975, he was beaten by Arthur Ashe in the quarter-finals at Wimbledon; Ashe, of course, went on to win the tournament. It was the last match Borg lost at Wimbledon until the final of 1981: 41 matches and all but six years without defeat. There are people who still can't quite believe it.

Borg was a master of topspin. As such, he invented the modern style of tennis, with a then unconventional double-fisted backhand. But Borg did it with wooden rackets: it wasn't until the synthetic rackets came in that people with less talent were able to play this way. With a wooden racket, strung tight as a snare drum, there was no forgiveness of even the minutest error in timing. Borg had invented this style of hitting with a racket his father had given him – a racket he had won in a ping-pong tournament, of all things – against the garage wall. His mature style was based on the idea that the racket was still too heavy for him: jerky, forced, wristy.

Borg first won Wimbledon in 1976, in an astonishingly hot summer – the final was played with peak temperatures of 41 degrees – in which the courts got baked hard. The ball sat up for Borg, which helped his baseline style. That was just the start. In 1976, he beat Illie Nastase in straight sets. At one moment, Nastase, frustrated and angry, deliberately hit a ball straight at him. Borg at once became a statue. He stood there, like a troll at sunrise, and stared Nastase down. The old reprobate was mortified. Borg won in straight sets. In 1978, 1979 and 1980, Borg won both the French Open and Wimbledon: antithetical surfaces, the same precision, the same temperament.

The final he is remembered for best is 1980. That was against the upstart McEnroe. "I never acted like a jerk against him," McEnroe said. "I had too much respect." By any logic, McEnroe should have won this match. He won the first set with all his most glorious talent on show, and was cruising the second set. But Borg somehow stole the big points. Great tennis players tend to be great because they play the big points better. It has been said of Borg that he was great because he didn't play the big points any differently. He played big points as if they were routine; he somehow took the breathless significance of them out of the equation and simply played the damn ball. After that, McEnroe, in disbelief, surrendered the third. But he was back to full power in the fourth.

It was McEnroe, not Borg, who had the best of that tie-break for which they will both always be remembered. It ended the fourth set, which bought them to two sets all; Borg saved six set points, McEnroe saved five championship points. And McEnroe won it. He won the greatest ever tie-break 18-16. By every logic in the emotional dramas of tennis, McEnroe should have gone on to win the match and the championship.

So Borg came out and played as if it was just another set, and McEnroe, whose style was to ride the mood-swings of his volatile nature, simply couldn't cope with that. Borg won the final set and the championship and was there on his knees once again: the man and his emotions making a touching reunion in the privacy of the Centre Court.

The match had seemed like a battle for the world: or at least, a battle for the world I wanted to live in. Borg was the hippy who fought against the punks, not that McEnroe was ever a punk in any demanding sense of the term. Nor was Borg much of a hippy, but at least he looked like one, and could be taken as an apostle for the hippy way. There were elements of the morality play about all this: and of course, the following year, McEnroe beat Borg in the final, and again in the final of the US Open. In January 1983, at the age of just 26, Borg retired. McEnroe said later he lived and played on "in continued mourning for Borg".

So, in a sense, did I. The hippy dream had gone. I had to deal with the world, and all its unpleasantness, as best I could.

19. Mike Brearley

THE ENGLISH HAVE A mystical belief in leadership; Mike Brearley is the ultimate expression of that belief. It's there in the numbers: a batsman not worth his place in the team, a captain with a quite stunning winning record. Brearley played in 39 Tests and has a batting average of 22.8; he was captain in 31 Tests, winning 17 and losing just four.

England loves a leader. The captain is the first name written down on the England team-sheet. The Australians take another view: they pick the best 11 cricketers and make one of them captain. The English make a big deal even of the England football captain; the Italians give the job to the player with the most caps, generally the goalkeeper. His job is to toss the coin at kick-off. The England football captain's job is to inspire by word and example.

Brearley was the embodiment of the English belief that leaders are worth a place in the team for their leadership qualities alone. Brearley was always hated and ridiculed by the Australians: after all, they're all mates together, an egalitarian society in which if you don't sit in the front, the taxi-driver will ask you "What's the matter, do I stink?" The Australians saw Brearley as insufficiently macho: a non-performer, an insult to their blokish egalitarian principles. They didn't buy into the notion that he was there to lead.

I did. Brearley went to Australia in 1979 and beat the Australians, all through the power of his leadership. It helped that he had David Gower, Ian Botham and Bob Willis in the team, but I was in no mood to quibble. I preferred the theory that he bought the best out of them all. Eventually, my belief in Brearley and his powers of leadership won me so much money I was able to pay my bar bill.

At the time, I was living on an island 45 minutes by ferry from Hong Kong. My neighbour, Al, was Australian. He gave me a great deal of grief about the Ashes series of 1981: England were a match down, the captain, Botham, got a pair at Lord's and walked back into the pavilion to the silence of the unapplauding members. Captaincy had broken him. He was not a leader. Instead, his attempt at leadership had destroyed his other abilities. He resigned: he would have been sacked had he not.

They tempted Brearley out of retirement: as captain, what else? It was a temporary measure, just to the end of the Ashes series. I was overjoyed. I knew at once that everything would be all right. It was because Brearley was back that I proposed a bet. Al offered me 150 dollars to 80 for England to win the Ashes. My winnings all but covered my debt to Ah-Chuen, who ran the island's al fresco bar among the vegetable gardens.

England won because Botham was reborn, remade, reinspired. In that first match, England followed on, but Botham scored 149 not out and Willis bowled Australia out for 111. With bat and ball, Botham harried the Australians in match after match. He forced them from a position of total dominance to one of abject defeat.

As a result, Brearley's already lofty reputation for leadership was made for all time. His book, *The Art of Captaincy*, reinforced that. It is compulsory reading for everyone who has followed him into that treacherous appointment. He takes with him his own personal cliché; it came from an Australian, oddly enough. Rodney Hogg, fast bowler, said: "He has a degree in people."

As chance would have it, I found myself some years later writing *A Singular Man*, a biography of Phil Edmonds, the England spin bowler. He and Brearley had been at variance at Middlesex and with the England team. Two Cambridge-educated men, both priding themselves on their intellect, both in some sense having the same act, both, in another sense, projecting widely different acts. Brearley had the quicker mind and was more verbally adroit; Edmonds had a more effective grasp of business and the world of affairs. They were well matched.

From Edmonds I heard a good deal about Brearley's failings, which initially seemed to me like a kind of blasphemy. Brearley, very sportingly – I think ultimately in a bad-tooth-biting way – agreed to see me for an interview for the book. Brearley saw this, perhaps rightly, as an adversarial situation. It is one of his basic tenets: "Try to reply to criticism with your intellect, not your ego." So he wasn't friendly. I was impressed by his coldness, his sense of certainty, his intellectual contempt for some of Edmonds' problems with him. I was also impressed by the way he willingly confessed that his dealings with Edmonds represented a personal failure. If Edmonds had failed, so had he.

Edmonds revisited all those years of strife with me; at one stage he seized Brearley by the shirt-front during the tea interval at a Test match in Australia to tell him: "Get off my back, Brearley, or I'll fucking fix you." But he found himself, almost despite himself, talking about Brearley's essential hardness. This was something the Australians missed. There was a one-day international. The Australians had wanted the match to be played with an innovation, fielding restrictions. Brearley refused, not because he thought it was a bad principle, but because he had not been given notice of these proposals. He got a savaging in the press for this. So then came the last ball, with Australia needing a boundary. Brearley put every man, wicketkeeper included, back on the fence – knowing that he would be booed and bollocked by the entire Australian nation.

That hardness, that coldness, that self-certainty was at the heart of his leadership. One of the points about Brearley was that though he was an intellectual with an impressive academic achievement, he had a deep respect for every kind of intelligence, cricketing intelligence in particular. There was never a vestige of intellectual snobbery. And he also had a taste for moments of gaiety and inspiration. He hated to let a game drift: at stagnant periods, he did things like putting himself on to bowl moon-balls, overarm lobs. He once even took a wicket: "John Emburey took the catch. I've never seen a man look so disgusted." He once took a fielder's helmet and placed it in the batsman's eyeline as a target, knowing that if the helmet was struck, it would cost five runs. The batsmen refused to go for it, to Brearley's disappointment, and the ploy was subsequently outlawed.

There was an occasion, shortly after the publication of *A Singular Man*, when by chance, Edmonds and I found ourselves in the same train carriage on the way to a Test match up north. Then Brearley walked in. It was a meeting both men would have avoided. But now, it was impossible, without gross discourtesy, to avoid a conversation lasting two and half hours. So we all sat together and the two of them had that conversation, with very little rancour, and a tacit admission was made that each represented the other's greatest failure in the sporting life.

I have been writing about sport for a long time since my artless 150-buck endorsement of Brearley and his power of leadership. I am sure now that Brearley's leadership wouldn't have worked in an Australian side. That's because being led implies an act of faith, and Australians are culturally inclined to resist it. But in England, where we believe in leadership, leadership can work very well indeed. The point is that leadership doesn't work without a sense of followership. And I must confess that I loved the idea of an intellectual winning cricket matches by the power of the mind.

If I am less overwhelmed by the Brearley myth than I was, it is only because I have watched a good deal of sport, written a great deal about sport and read a great deal about sport. It is important for everyone in sport to read Brearley. He said, "It is tempting to see events as not only inevitable but morally appropriate." That, in a line, is sportswriting. Sport itself is a good deal more complicated. Certainly, I saw those extraordinary Tests of 1981 as both inevitable and morally appropriate. It was with the joy of perfect righteousness that I handed my money to Ah-Chuen. And started a new tab.

20. Fiji

IT WAS TOWARDS THE end of the 70s when I moved to Hong Kong for a bit of an adventure. A couple of months later, it got a lot more adventurous. I was sacked by the *South China Morning Post*. A week after that, I had my first freelance assignment. I was off and away: an Asian freebooter, a gonzo journalist plying my trade for money or aeroplane tickets, charging around Asia, doing my own thing in my own time, taking on mad stories, smacking the deadline right in the middle, moving with a swagger and slouch, a stratospheric jaywalker with a notebook full of tales. I was a maverick winner in a constrained and buttoned-up world.

That, at any rate, was how I saw myself on my good days. That sacking was – no irony intended here – the greatest professional step of my career. It was intended as an eternal rebuke for my unworthiness: it turned out to be the gift of freedom. I have never recovered.

A year or so later, when I had a certain reputation around the publications of the region – he *always* delivers – I got a commission from a magazine called, I think, *Outdoors*. They asked me to "cover the Sevens". I had to go to the Hong Kong Rugby Sevens tournament. It was the first sporting assignment I had taken on since leaving England, and it was a revelation.

At that time, the Hong Kong Sevens was a relatively small deal. It was held in the football stadium, cosy and intimate and full of a few thousand hard-drinking expats. There were teams from all kinds of unlikely places, especially Fiji. I saw Fiji play and was at once entranced. Rugby, played the English way, is a safe and solid sort of sport, played by the safe and solid sort of good ol' English boys. It's all heads down and into the mud together, loads of merry old physical contact, bags of male camaraderie and what's done on the pitch stays on the pitch. We were supposed to play it at school: I avoided it at every opportunity.

Seven-a-side rugby is all about running and passing and tackling: open, fluid, a game custom-built for the inventive, the creative, the people with flair. The Fijian side, all seven of them, took that as a licence for madness. One-handed passes, behind-the-back passes, no-look passes, between-the-legs passes: all joined together with evasive running, dummies, trickery, sidesteps and stutter steps. And speed. Each man was an athlete with hands like butterfly nets and arms like bazookas. For the Fijians, rugby was a game of wit, invention, style. There are a million people in Fiji; 80,000 of them are regular players of rugby. This is one of the few nations of the world in which rugby union really is the national sport. The classic image is of children playing barefoot beach rugby with a coconut.

And here's a strange thing. Fiji were Hong Kong's boys. Fiji was the team everybody shouted for. The good ol' boys who made up the Hong Kong team were cheered dutifully as they laboured their way to an early knockout. But it was Fiji everybody really cared about. Fiji played for the Hong Kong spirit.

For a start, they were the most likely opposition to the teams from Australia and New Zealand, who naturally had to play the part of villains. But there was more to it than that. The maverick nature of the Fiji team reflected the maverick nature of Hong Kong itself. Back then, Hong Kong was a geopolitical maverick. It was a raging anachronism, a Chinese city that was part of China yet not part of China, full of wild brilliant Chinese entrepreneurs, a place where sky-reaching buildings went up more or less overnight, where everyone was working on some kind of deal, where crowds gathered in the street when the stock market and the gold prices were displayed outside the Hong Kong and Shanghai Bank, where everyone was living on his wits, in defiance of Europe, in defiance of China, in defiance of the whole world.

I became a Hong Kong freebooter with my sacking: but throughout the territory, we all saw ourselves – the British expats, the Chinese, the bohos, the chancers and the drunks – at least in some measure as adventurers. And the mad Fijian freebooters summed up the way we saw ourselves: taking on all the big guns of the world with wit, a pass that came from nowhere and a sidestep from God.

I went to the Sevens every year after that, and cheered for Fiji as a matter of patriotic duty, for I saw myself as a patriot of the nation of adventurers. When I returned to England, I was several times invited back to cover the event for *The Times*. I remember 1984 in particular. New Zealand had been thrown out of the competition because they had adopted the policy of sending out a series of half-baked provincial sides, who took it all as a jolly, a free plane ticket and a chance to catch up on their drinking. They were invited back when they offered to send a proper grown-up All Black side, a full international team, and naturally, their ambition was to show us what we had been missing. They invented a new muscular version of sevens, one based on conservative play, forward might and very rapid straight-line runners. They were going to win by means of power.

They got to the final, where they met Fiji. Before the final kicked off, a bunch of shirtless drunken Kiwis leapt onto the pitch to perform a seriously bad Haka. The Fijians glared at them. And then, as one man, they rocked into a war dance of their own, something I had never seen them do before. And then they played. They reached beyond themselves to produce the apotheosis of Fijian sevens: the ultimate expression of the entire concept of seven-a-side rugby. As a result, they gave New Zealand the rugby lesson of their lives. Power will get you so far, but wild artistry will get you further.

They won 26-0. Everything they tried came off. Every pass found a hand, and generally one huge hand was all that was necessary to snag it. Passes came from over the head, or between the ankles. Sleight of hand, sleight of foot. The All Blacks were, in the immortal words of Brendan Behan, bewitched, bollixed and bewildered. It was a triumph for Fiji, a triumph for Hong Kong, a triumph for the maverick spirit of the world.

Fiji's brilliance has never translated to the 15-a-side game. One of the problems is that most of the best individuals end up playing for Australia and New Zealand. Waisale Serevi didn't go that route, and remains the most brilliantly elusive runner I have ever seen. But it is the spirit of a nation I must celebrate here. Fiji have played the Hong Kong Sevens since 1976 and they have won it nine times; they have won the Sevens World Cup twice. Every victory was my victory. I took the path less travelled, largely because the *South China Morning Post* gave me no choice. I was bullied and forced into freedom: the Fijian seven-a-side rugby team embodied, ferociously, the freedom I had been unable to escape.

1980s

21. Ian Botham

THERE COMES A MOMENT when you realise that the great athletes performing before your enthralled eyes have changed. Suddenly – without warning – they are younger than you. Is it possible to have a hero younger than yourself? Do you not lose all dignity when conferring heroic status on someone who was an oiky schoolboy when you were already strutting about the world as a grown-up?

Only if you believe heroes require worship and blind adoration. Only if you need to see your hero as a perfect being. Sport does call on rather basic responses, but basic doesn't have to mean infantile. Sport can also be a legitimate part of grown-up life. In sport, we see ancient mythic patterns forming in modern-day competition: its heroes, people we are increasingly capable of seeing as flawed, prone to alarming lapses, hag-ridden by fear and set about by failure, yet people who are still capable of performing inspirational deeds. As such, they play a wholly legitimate role in the way grown-ups understand the world.

So no, I didn't see Ian Botham as a god stepped down to earth, I saw him as a man. A remarkable one, but one whose flaws were as much a part of him as his soaring achievements. A little over four years younger than me, he nonetheless represented a different generation. For me he was, I suppose, the hero on the cusp. Certainly, he laid down a series of per-formances that inspired an uncritical boyish delight, while at the same time he was clearly a person I could measure more coolly, with a more than half-formed adult eye.

In point of fact, Bjorn Borg, already mentioned in these pages, is younger than Botham. But somehow, he seemed dif-ferent. His greatest achievements came in a different decade.

In looks, in haircut, in personal style, Borg seemed more like a contemporary than a youngster. As Botham hit the greatest heights of his career in that unforgettable summer of 1981, it was the first time a person from an obviously different generation claimed a place in my panheroikon.

Botham had been England captain. I laugh, now, when I hear him in the commentary box chiding other former England captains about their records, about their past mistakes. No one ever dares to ask: well, Beefy, what was your record as captain? Answer: Played twelve, eight draws, four defeats. Wins nought. In his defence, I must point out that nine of his twelve matches were against the West Indies, who were unbeatable by anyone at the time. All the same, it is a record that takes a bit of laughing off.

His great disadvantage as captain was that he wasn't – like Mike Brearley – able to call on himself. That's because captaincy undermined his concentration and his confidence, his swagger and his self-certainty. Captaincy unmanned him. In short, by putting Botham in charge, England got a poor captain while simultaneously losing their best player. The same mistake was made with Andrew Flintoff for the Ashes tour of 2006–7.

Botham captained England for the first two Tests of the 1981 series against Australia, losing one of them. He then resigned. Brearley took over. Things went no better in the third Test at Headingley. Australia declared on 401 for nine, England were all out 175. Botham took six wickets, and then made a 50, his first since his first Test as captain, but England were still a long way second best. They were asked to follow on, and bookmakers offered odds of

500-1 on an England victory.

When England were 41 for four, the bookies must have been counting their money. At 135 for seven, it was surely all over. That's when Botham asked Graham Dilley, the fast bowler coming out to bat at number nine, if he fancied batting for two days on a difficult pitch. "No way." "Then let's give it some humpty."

It was Dilley who began to hit out first, Dilley who was prime mover of the miracle, playing some axe-murderer cuts off the front foot. But then Botham got the measure of the tiring Australian attack and started to help himself. Dilley made 56, Chris Old, coming in next, made 28. Botham made his century; the television cameras caught Brearley applauding from the players' balcony, and then pointing urgently out to the middle: stay there! It's no longer just about your fun!

Botham made 149 not out, England had a lead of 130, and with it, the faintest whiff of half a chance. Botham, man of the hour, bowled, but without magic. So Bob Willis came back on, having groused about having to bowl into the wind. And then, in the spell of his life, took eight for 43, and one of the most dramatic and unlikely Test matches in history was won.

England were in a losing position again in the following match. Australia, needing 150 to win, were 105 for five. For once, Botham had shown reluctance to bowl, arguing that the wicket would better suit others, but Brearley talked and teased him into it. John Emburey was bowling off-spin at the other end. Brearley told him: "Keep it tight for Embers." Botham did that all right. He took the last five wickets for one run in a glorious outpouring of the will.

In the match after that, Botham played a better innings than the one he did at Headingley, a withering, almost contemptuous 118, repeatedly and memorably hooking Dennis Lillee off his eyebrows, some feat in those helmet-less days. The commentator Richie Benaud said: "And that ball's gone into the confectionery stand and out again."

Botham, the deposed captain, the lost leader, the man who had forgotten how to bat and bowl, was man of the match on each of those three occasions, and of course, man of the series. These were the three matches that defined him for ever: a man of inspiration, a man who rises to great occasions, a man made for the epic of sporting surprise.

For the rest, well, he was indisputably a great player, an all-rounder whose batting average, 33.54, was higher than his bowling average, 28.4. He scored a century and had five wickets in an innings in five Test matches: only three men have done this more than once, and none of them more than twice.

As the 80s unwound, Botham's form began to fall away and he lost his ability to swing the ball late at pace. He was still the biggest name in British sport, at a time when football was in steep decline. He went through turbulence and scandal, but he – and his marriage – survived.

He is among a handful of heroes in this book whom I know personally. Not well, but he is a man of vast affability, who will make you his best friend for five minutes as he passes and leave you better pleased with the day. I have written some hard things about him when it has seemed necessary, but Botham seems to have no trouble with that. We have raised a glass on a couple of occasions when we have found ourselves in the same hotel, drank cups of tea at cricket venues where television and newspaper people are unsegregated and share the same space for refreshments. He is capable of filling a room with good vibes, especially if there is a bar in it. He clapped me massively round the shoulders the last time our paths crossed: it seemed odd, for a moment, that the hero of Headingley should do such a thing to me.

But I must close with my favourite Botham story, told by another ex-pro-turned-media-person, Simon Hughes. In his excellent book *A Lot of Hard Yakka*, Hughes talks about an evening with Botham, briefly his team-mate at Durham. They were sharing a bottle of wine after a meal; the first voice is Botham's.

"Can you bring me some dolecetti?" he asked. The waiter looked blank.

"Don't you mean dolcelatte?" I intercepted.

"That's what I said, dolecetti," he repeated.

"No, it's *dolcelatte*," I insisted, rather labouring the point.

There was a slight pause while he absorbed the information. Then he snapped: "Well, how many bloody Test wickets did you get?"

22. Shergar

1981. WHAT A YEAR. Shergar won the Derby, Botham won the Ashes, I met a girl and reader, I married her. I proposed and was accepted within a week; I won my cricket bet thanks to Brearley and Botham; I bet 20 quid on Shergar. You could say that I came out a winner.

Shergar was misnamed. His real name was Pegasus. I never saw him during his racing career, either in the flesh or on television, but from what I heard, it was obvious that he had wings. It was the only explanation. He won the Guardian Classic Trial by ten lengths: as if he was running in a completely different race, as if he represented a different order of being. He won the Chester Vase by 12 lengths. It was clear that this was one of the greatest racehorses that had ever set his proud hooves on the receiving earth. And so to the Derby.

How I loved the Derby. The race had a mythical resonance for me. I had been, once, and sat out on Epsom Downs, free in those days, with a packet of sandwiches and a can of beer. I bet on a loser while Shirley Heights came through on the rails and took out Hawaiian Sound in the last couple of strides. (Shirley Heights was trained by John Dunlop; a few years later, I spent a year in Dunlop's yard researching a book.) The Derby represented the ultimate sporting achievement, the greatest prize of them all, for I was besotted by racing. I bought the *Sporting Life* every day, read all the stuff in six-point type, tried to conjure a winner from the wonderfully arcane ink marks. And it all culminated in the Derby.

I tried to keep in touch with English racing when I moved to Hong Kong, at least to some extent, and the tales of Shergar hit me very deep. So I rang my parents, partly from duty but mainly to ask my sister's boyfriend to bet £20 – a week's rent – on Shergar to win the Derby.

The race wasn't shown on Hong Kong television, of course. I listened to the commentary on the World Service, the sneering patrician tones of Peter Bromley. It was just after midnight. Cindy, now my fiancée, was beside me. We listened to the progression across to the downs and the starting gate, to the information that Walter Swinburn, the 19-year-old jockey, was on board. They started. Shergar seemed to be placed handily. They came to Tattenham Corner. Shergar took the lead – and at once Bromley's voice soared above the stave, hitting high notes that the torrid airwaves simply couldn't sustain. For four furlongs, I heard nothing but a kind of hysterical hiss. "That stupid boy, he's gone too early, he's been caught," I wailed aloud. And then Bromley's voice descended to calmer levels: "And Shergar… has won the Derby… with *ridiculous* ease."

Ah, the joy of it. The speed, the directness, the brilliance, the joy. Life had assumed a new simplicity for me: I was with Cindy and nothing else mattered, nothing else at all. All that it took to make it work, I would do. And something in this arrow-straight flight, this simple directness, this shattering, all-consuming victory, seemed to be an emblem of what my life should be.

Shergar's was not the victory of the underdog, the lone maverick taking his chance, the reckless intuitive punt that somehow might just come off. No: it was the cool logic of the overdog, the runaway favourite, the obvious, the logical, the only possible winner. There was no other solution to the conundrum of the race than Shergar: there was no answer to the puzzle of life but Cindy. I too was a runaway favourite. I had become a racing certainty. I was so much a winner that no other possibility mattered even remotely.

Though as a matter of fact, John Matthias thought he'd won as he rode towards the winning post. "I told myself I'd achieved my life's ambition. Only then did I discover there was another horse on the horizon." He was so far second he hadn't seen the winner. Swinburn was applauded back to the winner's circle: he just pointed to the horse. A few months later, I was to repeat that gesture when I carried off some small prize in showjumping. Swinburn said later: "Shergar found his own pace and lobbed along as the leaders went off at a million miles an hour with me just putting my hand down his withers and letting him travel at his own speed."

He won by ten lengths, the widest winning margin in the history of the Derby. He went on to win the Irish Derby in what Peter O'Sullevan, the BBC television commentator, described as "an exercise canter". He then took on the older horses in the King George VI and Queen Elizabeth Stakes and beat the lot. His racing career ended with an anticlimax, fourth in the St Leger.

I'm half reluctant to tell the rest of the tale. Normally, when a hero comes to a sticky end, it has an air of inevitability about it, the flaws that made for greatness eventually bringing about the downfall. That was not the case with Shergar. He was retired from the racetrack and went to stand at stud in Ireland. There, he was taken by, it is believed, the Provisional IRA, who later killed him. There was an attempt to contact the Aga Khan and demand a ransom, but this was never paid, not least because the Aga Khan was no longer sole owner, having sold 34 of the 40 shares in the horse after the King

George. It seems the IRA had overlooked this detail, and besides, there was the feeling that if kidnapping stallions was shown to be a profitable business, the entire thoroughbred breeding industry would be in danger of collapse.

Certainly, Shergar was killed, probably very soon after the kidnapping. A thoroughbred stallion is a difficult animal to look after, being both delicate, flighty and occasionally aggressive. Some believe that Shergar was shot within hours of his capture. All in all, the kidnapping of Shergar was an almighty cock-up: not the way a hero should meet his end.

Shergar left just 35 foals, the best of which was Authaal, who won the Irish St Leger. We will never know what might have been. But it's the Derby that matters in the story of Shergar. The race was his destiny, his long moment of perfection. On Epsom Downs he took wing as no horse had ever done before: a bright bay horse with a white face, the boy on his back wearing green and red, moving past the others as if it was the easiest, the most natural, the most inevitable thing in the world, as swallows fly past sparrows. This was a moment of perfect certainty, and it was my mood too as the year of 1981 unfolded.

23. Torvill and Dean

IS ICE DANCE A FLAWED sport or a flawed art? Probably both. The thing that separates sport from art – specifically, performance art – is control. The ballerina playing Odile knows she will be able to perform the famous 32 fouettes: she won't fall down. But in figure skating – which is a different discipline from ice dance – you have jumps, and when you perform a triple Axel, you must enter the jump at speed, make three and a half revolutions in the air, and then land with a nice flowing edge on a frightfully slippery surface. This is not something for which you can offer a 100 per cent guarantee. Even at the highest level – Olympic competition – you regularly see falls and errors even among the greatest. The performers all go into every competition unsure whether or not they will come out without ice in their knickers. No big jump is a matter of complete certainty, and that is what tips the balance towards sport rather than art. But ice dance has none of these risks. There are no jumps. A fall is very rare. Ice dance exists on the safe side of control and that makes it bad art rather than bad sport.

How, then, can we explain Torvill and Dean? How can we explain the fact that they were magnificent, spell-binding, compelling? How can we explain the fact that so many people, many of them equally used to great art and great sport, found something to marvel at in the strange, intense, kitsch, gold-medal-winning performance of Jayne Torvill and Christopher Dean?

They began at Nottingham ice rink. She was an insurance clerk, he was a police cadet. It's fair to say that even when they were at the towering peak of their sporting lives, they looked like an insurance clerk and police cadet from Nottingham.

But that was part of the magic: perhaps even the most important part. Their transfiguration came from within.

They won their first world championship with a free dance to a traditional medley of songs, but the following year, they went in with higher ambitions, not just to win but to put something of themselves into the performance and into the sport itself. So they performed a free dance with a theme and a narrative, a performance based on the musical *Mack and Mabel*, a story in dance about a sardonic love affair. The following year they won the world championship with a dance based on *Barnum*, in which the circus was recalled in their dance with wit and style. Even at this stage, they wanted to do more than score points. They were – in this absurd medium – looking for something deeper. Looking to express something that went beyond themselves and their skating skills.

Their partnership rose to new levels of ambition with an inspirational friendship with Michael Crawford, the actor who took the title role in the stage production of *Barnum*. He encouraged them to step still further from the constraints of competitive skating: to look for the art that lay beyond it. He taught them to act: he taught them about an emotional commitment that goes beyond the physical commitment that is native to all the great performers in sport. Torvill and Dean were used to chasing perfection in a way that far surpasses any performance artist's achievements: for Torvill and Dean, every small flaw in performance would be cold-heartedly assessed and marked. The search for sporting – as opposed to artistic – perfection involves hour after hour on the ice, going beyond pain and boredom and exhaustion, moving into a twilight that frays nerve ends and pushes relationships to their limits. Their shared desire for success, and the deep and certain knowledge that each needed the other, was the glue that kept them together. Not love, as the more sentimental commentators believed. Some years later, a documentary showed the two of them at practice, with Dean reducing Torvill to tears over the niggling details of perfection. This shocked a sentimental audience. It shouldn't have. How else did anyone think they had achieved perfection? Ice dance may be a flawed sport, but that doesn't stop it being seriously demanding, and savagely difficult.

Torvill and Dean reached their apotheosis in 1984, at the Winter Olympic Games in Sarajevo. After the compulsory dances, they were required to perform the short dance –the Original Set Pattern – and a paso doble was demanded. They stunningly interpreted this dance as a bullfighter with his cape, Torvill playing the inanimate cape to Dean's strutting matador. It was conceptually brilliant, and it was carried out with outrageous conviction. At the finale, Dean contemptuously flung his partner to the ground and left her spinning face down on the ice while he struck an attitude, a flourish of the arms and chin in the air. He still looked like a police cadet: yet the airs and the panache of the matador of fantasy penetrated every nuance of his performance, which was supported by an immaculate and nobly self-restrained performance from his partner.

Which led, of course, to the ineffable *Bolero*. Really, that dance should have been a hoot. It was nothing of the kind. They chose the music that had been used in the film *10* as a comedic accompaniment to casual sex. They wore costumes in staggered shades of mauve and purple. They did a dance about doomed lovers flinging themselves into a volcano. It should have been kitsch beyond belief, it should have been Tretchikoff's *Chinese Girl* on ice, it should have been the naff-est thing ever seen on television. But it wasn't. It was profoundly moving.

One reason for this was the emotional commitment they revealed in a performance that, even when viewed now, is filled with the lines of passion and despair. All the same, had they put on a similar performance on the stage in Notting-ham Town Hall with a half-baked dance routine, the whole thing would have been seriously embarrassing. The point is that the emotional commitment was allied to the technical perfection of their skating, the austerity of the one setting off the excess of the other.

For all that, it was not something that stood alone as great art. Without the scores, that row of nine perfect 6s for "artistic impression", it would not have had anything like the same resonance. Nor would the sport have meant so much to its patriotic viewers without the emotional nature of the performance. This was a strange hybrid, neither art nor sport, brought to life by those cuckoos in the nest of suburbia, a pair who took a strange and deeply kitsch medium and somehow created a thunderclap of genuine art and genuinely great sport.

I was by this time just beginning to write for *The Times*. I attended a reprise performance that they gave as newly fledged professionals, and reported on it; later, I was to report on their Olympic comeback.

There was something about Torvill and Dean that I

couldn't fail to relate to. They tried to bring art to a medium that was primarily competitive; I think now that this is what I have been trying to do myself. Though their job was to win gold medals, they couldn't help but try and smuggle art into it. They were unable to perform cynically, for marks alone. Instead, they had to bring total commitment. They had to bring their entire selves into the task in hand, not just their competitive natures. In a medium unsuitable for high art they gave all they could. Sportswriting is probably an equally un-suitable medium for artistic endeavour; nevertheless, to try and write without commitment seems to me not only a lie, but an activity devoid of meaning.

Torvill and Dean took something of questionable value and created from it art and sport: and both these things are of unquestionable value. Alchemy is the science of taking dross and creating from it pure gold. Torvill and Dean were alche-mists.

24. Malcolm Marshall

THERE IS NO SPORT without fear. There is no courage without fear. There are no heroes without fear. We celebrate those who have stood firm in the face of adversity; I have celebrated in these pages Colin Cowdrey and David Steele, who faced the greatest fast bowlers of their age.

But those who impart fear also have their heroic qualities. *The Wisden Cricketers' Almanack 2000* asked the great and the good of world cricket to nominate the greatest players of the 20th century. The top five comprised three batsmen, one batting all-rounder and one leg-spinner. No fast bowlers. It seems the great and the good were too squeamish to acknowledge the truth: that it's the fast bowlers who win most matches. If I was picking the team of the 20th century, the first name on my list would be Malcolm Marshall.

No one ever bowled fast with the sole aim of defeating the hand–eye coordination of the batsman. Every fast bowler ever spawned wants to extort a little fear. The greatest master of fear was Marshall. What he did was as terrible as it was magnificent. He took on the best and the bravest: he exposed their technical shortcomings and their failures of courage.

By 1984, I was starting to cover major sporting events for *The Times*. But I wasn't there at Edgbaston when Andy Lloyd had one of the shortest Test careers in history. He stepped out to open the batting for England against the West Indies in the first Test match. Seven overs later, he was on his way to hospital. He never played for England again. Fear had undone him. He misread the length of a ball from Marshall and, fearing a head-high bouncer, ducked. Alas, he ducked *into* the ball instead of under it. The ball was not all that short. It was Lloyd's wariness that caused his injury. The ball struck the side of his helmet; its protection was inadequate. Lloyd spent ten days in hospital; his vision was damaged. John Woodcock, writing as editor of *Wisden 1985*, said that the West Indies team of that year added "a new, and dare I say it, chilling dimension to the game".

England lost the first two Tests comprehensively. I managed to get to the third at Leeds. There, I saw the most outrageous exploitation of fear ever seen on a cricket field: and a craven capitulation. Or was it so craven? Perhaps I should not be harsh on England, for they came up against the master of fear.

In a bad situation, you look for hope, and when hope comes, it seems like a sign from on high. But when this fleeting hope is dashed, despair is ten times closer than before. That Saturday evening at Headingley, I witnessed despair. And it was Marshall's work.

Marshall broke his thumb while fielding during England's first innings. He had to leave the field; his arm was put into plaster. Obviously, he would take no further part in the match. You could almost see the prayers of thanksgiving rising from the England dressing room like white smoke from the Vatican chimney. England had been let off. True, they still had to face Garner and Holding, but the most terrible of them had gone. Marshall: wicket-less in a match. It seemed that the gods had suddenly relented.

When England took the ninth West Indian wicket, the total not much more than their own, they celebrated the end of the innings with Larry Gomes stuck on 96. The tide had surely turned. But it hadn't, you see: out came Marshall, left arm in plaster and a bat in his right hand. He batted one-handed, fending off the bowling while Gomes made his century; he also hit a four, one-handed, a kind of disguised forehand cross-court. Then he got out at last, and a peculiarly irritating sideshow was over. Still, obviously a man with his arm in plaster couldn't bowl.

At the break between innings, the West Indians did something they never normally do. They did a public warm-up. They went through a series of physical jerks right under the window of the England dressing room. And Marshall was among them. Surely this couldn't be.

The West Indian team returned to the pavilion and then came out to take the field. And Marshall was still among them. Marshall, with an air of undisguised relish. At a stroke, England's sense of relief turned into undisguised panic. Marshall took three wickets that evening as England collapsed to 135 for six, and he took the last four wickets on Monday morning, when he dropped his pace and swung the ball lavishly. Terror was only one of his weapons.

Marshall dominated a series that the West Indies won 5-0, one that became known as the Blackwash Summer. This was followed by a second Blackwash in the West Indies in 1986, in which England were reduced to a bickering rabble. Mike Gatting, struck in the face by a ball from Marshall, had to go home, horribly bruised, an unforgettable image of the modern England cricketer.

Marshall always saved his best for England. There was no more calypso cricket, no more happy-go-lucky stuff. This was reggae cricket: get up, stand up – stand up for your rights. It had a hard edge. It was cruel and yes, even chilling. Marshall was widely seen in England as a villain, a man who used unfair tactics – like speed and skill – against his moral betters. It was some years before he was recognised as a player of brilliance: one who had the courage to set about the established order and dominate.

He finished his career with 367 Test wickets. His average, 20.94, is the lowest of any bowler to take more then 200 wickets. Yet he was slightly built, all wire and whiplash. Most fast bowlers are tall men: Marshall was well under six feet. His bouncer didn't descend from a great height and jump: it skidded on from sheer unstoppable speed. Yet the bouncer was not his chief weapon. His chief weapon was speed: controlled speed. He could swing the ball, and later developed a devastating leg-cutter. He was a fast bowler with a complete armoury. Terror was only the most devastating part of his armoury, and the one most vividly remembered.

He was part of a devastating team: the West Indies side of the 1980s seemed to be an endless dynasty, with one destructive fast bowler following another, one destructive batsman taking the pace of the one before. I remember the West Indies at their height: perhaps the finest cricket team that ever stepped out of a pavilion. Some called them one-dimensional because they had little time for spin bowling, but that is mere chatter about aesthetics: the West Indies used their greatest weapons to win Test matches and destroy their opponents, and it was a magnificent and terrible sight. Marshall died of colon cancer at the age of 41. West Indies cricket has continued to decline since his retirement.

I was brought up in a liberal household, and equality was a thing we took for granted, but all the same, we were aware of our own largeness of heart, our own magnanimity, in conferring this equal status on black people. But out came Marshall, out came the West Indies team, to take a prolonged, magnificent revenge on us all. It was not even equality that this West Indies side represented, for there was no equality. England were blackwashed. This was superiority. This was a rout. The outcast, the underdog, had become master.

25. Martina Navratilova

SPORTS WRITING IS A MACHO profession. Sport it-self is still seen largely as an activity dominated by traditional male values. In December 2009, five *Times* sports columnists, all male, got together for a podcast debate on the subject of the top ten sporting moments of the decade just gone. I pointed out that the ten moments we were required to choose from included no women. "You're standing up for tokenism?" "No – completion." Cathy Freeman got in.

Sportswriting was even more macho when I joined the mainstream profession in the 1980s. For example, I found widespread contempt for Torvill and Dean: sport was only sport if it pleased macho sensibilities. When I started cov-ering Wimbledon, I found deeper problems. Men's tennis was just about allowable, but women's tennis met with com-plex responses. If the women were pretty they weren't proper athletes; if they were athletes they weren't proper women.

I don't want to be unfair on my colleagues here, nor do I want to claim that I was a lone dissenting voice. But there was a universal awkwardness about women in sport: an awkwardness seasoned with jokes. Into the middle of this came Martina Navratilova.

I have never had problems with the idea of strong women. As I have said, my mother was a feminist long before the term was invented. I read Germaine Greer's *The Female Eunuch* in 1970, the year it came out, and its breathtaking audacity had me nodding in total agreement. It changed the way a generation of people thought. This new and bracing book kicked all sorts of nonsense into touch. I was a stand-up-and-be-counted feminist at 20.

Professional sport was then, and still is, a male-dominated

business, at least in terms of financial reward and media coverage. These days, football is the bedrock of sports coverage but women's football scarcely gets a mention. Women's track and field athletes get space when there is a British star. Apart from that, outside of the Olympic Games, the only time women's sport has a high profile in British newspapers is during Wimbledon. Hardly surprising, then, that some sportswriters, those who are not tennis specialists, go to Wimbledon for an annual fix of tennis and find it hard to know how to deal with women's tennis, women's sport, with the entire phenomenon of high-achieving women. Sportswriting doesn't give you the practice.

In the 1980s, sportswriters didn't just have to deal with women. They had to deal with Navratilova. She won the Wimbledon singles title every year between 1982 and 1987. She brought to her sport levels of fitness and commitment never previously seen in the game. She invented the travelling entourage of tacticians, dieticians, playing partners and physical conditioners: Team Navratilova changed the face of tennis. In her career she won 18 grand-slam singles titles, along with 31 doubles and 10 mixed doubles. Altogether, she won 167 singles titles and 177 titles in doubles. She won the Wimbledon singles nine times.

It is almost compulsory for great stars of sport to become corporate properties. There is a fortune to be made in professional hypocrisy (it's technically known as "being a role model"). Tiger Woods, before his fall, perfected the art of speaking much while saying nothing and hiding everything. Michael Jordan refused to speak out on racial and political issues because "Republicans buy sneakers too". But when you asked Navratilova a question, she answered it. Honestly. No matter what the subject.

She told the world she was homosexual. The idea of hiding simply didn't occur to her. Not all my colleagues were entirely relaxed about this. She knew that by doing so, she was throwing away millions of corporate dollars, but she had no taste to play the part. She was born in Czechoslovakia, defected to the United States during the US Open when she was 18 and became a US citizen. She has never failed to criticise her adopted country when she found it necessary. When she has been told "go back to Czechoslovakia if you don't like it", she has consistently responded that freedom of speech is one of the privileges of being American. Ask her about human rights, gay rights, animal rights, any kind of rights at all, and she will have an honest and thought-out view, not a view designed to give her an advantage or to make her look good, but one that comes from conviction. People talk about conviction politicians: she is that rare, almost unique thing, a conviction athlete.

And the best. She had a long rivalry with Chris Evert, who was happy to play the pretty American Miss. Their rivalry was a fine thing that elevated both of them, but Navratilova, by means of longevity, by means of her demented fitness programme, dominated its latter stages.

She was a beguiling contradiction: masculine in terms of her pared-down physique, her commitment and her phenomenal all-court athleticism; feminine in terms of her emotional intensity, on court and elsewhere. She was prone to terrible mid-match wobbles: yet she was a champion beyond the reach of the rest.

And along with the outspoken honesty, she had a sense of humour and an uncompromising verbal intelligence. She was asked the difference between herself and her competitors. "They're involved. But I'm committed." "What's the difference, Martina? "It's like ham and eggs. The chicken's involved. But the pig's committed." She embodied another contradiction: a mad obsessive drive to win at sport and a sane and grounded understanding of real life. She was one of the first athletes to see that winning was a lifestyle choice, not something you do during working hours. Everything she did was geared towards winning: and yet she remained a fundamentally sympathetic person with an elevated idea of what a famous people ought to do and say.

I met her just once, shortly after she retired. We talked mostly about animal rights, a subject we both have opinions on. I was deeply struck by her face. I had last seen her when she was playing tennis at Wimbledon. But now, the lines of strain had gone. She had acquired the right to the last adjective I ever thought I would apply to her: serene. She and I are both patrons of Save the Rhino: alas, we have yet to make the same meeting, but I look forward to it when it comes.

Navratilova, in her playing pomp, represented all those things I learned to value when I was 20: things to do with freedom and honesty and the acknowledgment of the rights of other people, and other living things. Many felt threatened by Navratilova: me, I felt quite the reverse: supported, exalted, validated. Many people in this book stand for certain important things: Navratilova is close to unique in thinking them through and standing for what she believed in as a matter of conscious choice. She turned down millions because of her honesty; she won everything because of her total and absolute commitment. If I must choose a single hero to represent the entire concept of heroism in sport, let it be Martina.

26. David Gower

LIAQAT ALI. THAT WAS his name. He was the man who bowled David Gower's first ball in Test cricket. What followed is cricketing folklore: Gower, with that sweet bewildered expression, swat-pulled the ball for four.

How beautiful, how absurd, how sweet he looked, with that great unpermed head of curls: somewhere between Marilyn Monroe and Harpo Marx. How sweet his timing, how incomparably sweet: he had so much time to play the shot that he seemed to have a dozen different options. His movement was languid, his bat speed was lightning. Cricket was a different game for him.

Gower made his Test match debut against Pakistan in 1978; he was at his best in the early 1980s. This was the time I was establishing myself as a professional sportswriter. Naturally, a person who succeeded with so little apparent effort, with so much apparent genius, had a great deal to recommend him. But by this time I wasn't just looking for somebody to identify with. When I watched Gower, I was looking at a subject. A fabulous subject, a man with all the contradictions, a man who polarised views, a player some thought genius and others waster. Application versus flair: glory versus results: style versus substance: Roundhead versus Cavalier. Gower gave you a debate every time he strode out to bat. What writer could resist?

There was one shot in particular I loved and that I have never seen anyone else play. It was a sort of flick-pull. He seemed to twitch his bat through a perfunctory arc of 45 degrees, and the ball would scorch the grass all the way to the boundary. It is the supreme example of what cricket people call timing: the intersection of bat and ball at the precise instant that maximises the batsman's control over the speed and direction of the ball's subsequent journey. Much of modern batting is by means of the bludgeon, the heavy bat thrashed through the line of the ball on an easy wicket. Gower's technique was a thing that had you scratching your head in wonder: how could the ball travel so hard and so fast from such little effort? More than any batsman I have ever seen, Gower was able to conjure up the illusion of complicity. It looked as if bowler and batsman were collaborating in their attempts to make the ball fly so wondrously. It was as if they were performing a complex *pas de deux*, with movements long planned and thoroughly rehearsed, rather than acting out a bitter opposition.

It looked like magic. Years ago, I wrote a book of literary parodies on a cricket theme, *A la Recherche du Cricket Perdu*. There was a Tolkien pastiche: "The Tale of Lubo the Elf and Gatti the Dwarf", Lubo being one of Gower's nicknames. "I have my wand and do not doubt it can do some damage to the Enemy."

Gower was a great cricketer with a marvellous record: 8,231 runs came from his wand at an average of 44.24, with 18 centuries. Yet people believed he should have done still better. I was always on Gower's side myself, but I very rapidly learned that if you wish to support a genius, you're on your own. Certainly, you will get no help from the genius. Gower was never out of form. He always looked absolutely perfect, until he made a mistake. He never seemed to scratch about for runs, always looked calm and easy and sumptuously graceful. And then he'd have a waft – the word followed him almost as closely as his other inevitable cliché, laid-back – and, in the left-hander's great tradition, he'd touch a ball bowled across him to the slips.

He is man whose errors must always be celebrated alongside his successes, partly because so many stodgy and worthy figures had a terrible fascination for his mistakes, but also because Gower can't be explained outside the context of his errors. In the Ashes series of 1985, as England captain, he scored 732 runs at 81.33 as England won 3-1. In the celebrations afterwards, he said on camera: "I'm sure the West Indies are quaking in their boots", a facetiousness that was utterly characteristic, and which alienated as many as it charmed.

The former England selector Alec Bedser said: "He has disappointed a few people in not carrying on during certain innings. He should have applied himself more." People always like to say that a genius with a wayward streak should snap out of it and apply himself more. Why, then, is a good, steady, hard-working player never told to snap out of it and be a genius? People said Gower would be better if he put his mind to it: it seemed to me that Gower's basic strength was that he didn't put his mind to it. Rather, he gave himself up to his gift.

I got to know him a little during that time, interviewing him several times. He was easy, cheerful, funny, immensely likeable… and absolutely unknowable. He had considerable intelligence, but no taste for ideas. A good brain, but he shied away from any kind of analysis. Preferred a quip, a smile, move on, don't engage too deeply. He is now a television commentator, and so I bump into him at the cricket and he is always supremely agreeable… and supremely unknowable. I have a good deal in common with him. We share a great love of Africa and its wildlife – Gower was brought up in Tanganyika, now Tanzania. He is a patron of the World Land Trust, a charity that finances the purchase of endangered habitats; I am a council member. Yet despite this, there's always some bit of Gower that I, that most people, seem to be miss. Nothing could be easier than a nice chat with Gower: nothing could be harder than finding the man.

There is an evasive streak in him, one he has always dressed in facetiousness. He walked out of a press conference as England captain because he "had tickets for a play". He hired a Tiger Moth and had the pilot buzz the ground where England were playing – where he should have been dutifully watching. Not everybody took the jape well. Perhaps they took it in the spirit in which it was intended: as demonstration that there was something in Gower that didn't care in quite the same manner as everybody else.

Graham Gooch became England captain and never got the hang of Gower. Although a decent person and fine cricketer, Gooch was always a man short of imagination. He simply couldn't understand how Gower could have such skill, and yet have as many failures as successes. Gooch believed in work: he would sooner have a talented grafter than a flaky genius. So after Gower made one misjudgement too many, and was out in a Test match in Adelaide the last ball before lunch, Gooch had had enough. Gower was dropped for the tour of India under Gooch's captaincy in 1992–93. There was a protest and an attempt by MCC members to have this overturned, for Gower was always greatly loved by spectators, but it wasn't to be.

Gower retired the following summer: a man at the same

time frustrated and fulfilled. He was much despised and much loved. He was misunderstood, and yet he constantly evaded all attempts to understand him. He was the finest player of cricket shots I will ever see and he sometimes put these together to build some sumptuous Test match innings. Some say he let himself down, that he should have been better: me, I think he was exactly, but precisely as good as it was in his power to be. He was flawed, like all geniuses. In sport, we give the title of genius not to the most successful but to the greatest ball-players: George Best, Ronnie O'Sullivan, John McEnroe. Sometimes it seems that the weight of their genius overrides their ability to succeed at the game, the humdrum pursuit of victories and records. This was true of Gower. We are richer for his successes, we are richer for his failings. As a professional sportswriter – well, at least as professional as Gower ever was at cricket – I give daily thanks for such people who make the job not only fascinating and rewarding but possible.

27. Dancing Brave

THE HEROIC LIFE PROVIDES many examples of change: transformation: metamorphosis. Hamlet turns from ditherer to murderer; Odysseus's crew turn from men to swine; Bilbo Baggins turns from stodgy stay-at-home to adventurer; Clark Kent finds a phonebox and turns into Superman; Strawberry the cab-horse goes to Narnia and turns into Fledge, the father of all winged horses.

In sport these transformations can take place before your eyes. Ian Botham turned from champion to loser-captain, and then changed into a greater champion than ever before. But the greatest sporting metamorphosis I ever saw was in the suburbs of Paris in the early autumn of 1986. I left my hotel on the Avenue d'Iena, a place not far from the scene of some of my youthful adventures before my metamorphosis into adulthood, and walked through the Bois de Boulogne to Longchamp.

How proud I was to be doing such a thing; how nervous. This was my first official assignment abroad for *The Times*. My flights and my hotel were paid for by the newspaper. I was, at a stroke, a proper sports journo. It was another metamorphosis, and I was inclined to think a hell of a lot of myself as a result.

I was not to know that the event I was there to see would be one of the greatest pieces of sport that I, or for that matter anyone else, had ever seen. If I had never travelled another yard after that first trip, I could still claim to have witnessed one of the greatest detonations of brilliance in the entire history of sport. I was there for the Prix de l'Arc de Triomphe. I was there for Dancing Brave.

The Arc is, if you like, the European Cup final for racehorses, in which the three-year-olds – the horses that contest the Classics – take on the older horses with the season almost at its end. Dancing Brave was a fine horse with some searching questions left to answer. He was not quite as good as every--one had hoped. After all, he had failed to win the Derby.

Dancing Brave won two races as a two-year-old, then two more in the early part of 1986. He then won the first Classic open to colts, the 2,000 Guineas, and went into the Derby as favourite. The Guineas is a mile: the Derby is half a mile more, over the notoriously hilly and quirky Epsom track. Would he be able to keep up with the pace and still have enough of that famous speed at the end of the race? He did. He came with a storming late run, much faster than Shahrastani at the front. But he never caught him. He was a fraction too late in his big move, and lost by half a length while travelling like a bolt of lightning. Some blamed the jockey, Greville Starkey; others said that Dancing Brave had trouble with the hills and dips of the track, and took a stride or so extra to respond to the request to quicken. Either way, he was second, which made him a loser.

Dancing Brave went on to win the Eclipse and the King George VI and Queen Elizabeth Stakes. By this time, Starkey had lost the ride and Pat Eddery had taken over. And it was clear that Paris, and the race with all the finest horses in Europe, was to be the ultimate examination of Dancing Brave's credentials for greatness.

The most excellent racing writer Brough Scott tells a story about the parade ring before the race. There was the owner, Prince Khalid Abdullah, and the trainer, Guy Harwood. Eddery walked into the ring with the air of a man wondering whether to get a magazine or a cup of coffee before he caught his train. Eddery had such a great reputation at this time that the idea of giving him "orders" was not really on, not even for princes or trainers of Harwood's stature. Eddery said nothing, and eventually Harwood lost his nerve and asked: "So what are you going to do, Pat?" Eddery, looking vague, muttered: "Oh… I think I'll hold him up a bit." That's what he did.

The race defies belief. Even when watching it again, I can't believe Dancing Brave is going to win. Even after he has done so, I can't believe that any horse could ever have been that good. Off they went, right-handed, round the generous curves of the racetrack, all the finest racehorses in training and – oh, there he is, right at the back, with only two or three horses behind him, way off the pace. And on they gallop, ferociously quick, towards the finish and by this time Dancing Brace… is still out at the back. Still cruising along enjoying a nice mellow fruitful autumnal afternoon.

Then with less than half a mile to go, there was the Brave. Eleventh of 15 runners. Ahead of him, poised to strike, Shardari, Darara, Shahrastani, all in the green colours of the Aga Khan. Behind them, Triptych and Bering. Bering took up an ominous position, clearly ready to make the race's decisive move. And Eddery… tucked Dancing Brave back inside. It was as brave a thing as I've ever seen in sport.

Then the post was upon them and all the niceties were forgotten and all the tactics were at an end and it was a straightforward uncomplicated blast for the post and for glory. I remember, up in the stands with a perfect view, seeing the Aga Khan's horses in a wall of three, surely impassable, surely about to carve the race up between then, but then I saw Bering, going faster still, swooping round on the outside to take the race in a magnificent burst of speed and power and wonderful timing.

Then, and only then, came Dancing Brave. Bering was the ace: Dancing Brave trumped him: trumped him derisively. Bering was fast: Dancing Brave made him look as if he was standing still. In that last furlong, Dancing Brave passed a dozen horses. It was as if he had metamorphosed, like Fledge, to become the father of all winged horses. In one instant, in one stride, Dancing Brave became Flying Brave, transformed in a couple of strides into the greatest race horse that ever looked through a bridle.

Behind me, I heard someone say: *"Quelle course! Quel jockey! Quel cheval!"* I knew I'd use that. You don't have to make things up in sports journalism: reality, to use the term loosely, invariably plays into your hands. Here was greatness. You don't have to take my word for it: Dancing Brave was given the highest ever rating by the racing people: 141, higher even than Shergar. This was a quite astonishing horse. Scott calculates that Dancing Brave was travelling as fast in the last quarter of the race, which took place over 2,400 metres, as Europe's top sprinter managed in a race of a mere 1,000 metres.

It was that quickening that stayed with me, that moment of metamorphosis. There wasn't a sense of identification with him: I may have had a bit of a metamorphosis myself, what with the plane ticket and the hotel and all, but I didn't think I had turned into Superman, still less the greatest writer ever with a rating of 141. What mattered was that my own transformation had given me the privilege of watching Dancing Brave and the still greater privilege of writing about him. For me, that was glory enough. I now had a professional life before me in which I could chart the course of heroes, and look for those moments of metamorphosis, those moments when athletes reveal themselves as – or transform themselves into – competitors of genuine greatness. As heroes. I was now an official chronicler of heroes. I had a panheroikon from the earlier part of my life to compare them with and an unknown panheroikon still to come. In the process of assembling it, my notions of greatness and heroism would develop and change and would themselves undergo a continuous metamorphosis.

28. Ben Johnson

BEN JOHNSON WAS THE lightning streak at noon and the thunderbolt in the dead of night. I was at my first Olympic Games, in Seoul in 1988, the lowliest member of Team *Times* in every opinion save my own, squeezing onto the plane thanks to a late change of heart from Tom Clarke, the sports editor. I was just one – but probably the most awestruck – of 10,000 or so journalists chronicling the doings of 10,000 or so athletes. I had never seen sport on such a scale. In the preliminaries, before the Opening Ceremony, I attended ferocious massed press conferences for Carl Lewis, the aloof, self-regarding American sprinter who had won four gold medals at the previous Games in Los Angeles, and for Florence Griffith-Joyner, who had set a new world record for the 100 metres at the United States Olympic Trials. As soon as the action began, I got involved with the Great Britain hockey team. And I filled in everywhere I could. I was fascinated by the scale of the Games, but more than that, by the meaning of the Games. This was not something I had considered before. The Olympic Games are about a single chance. At the very best, one chance in four years: for most, it comes down to one chance in a lifetime. Everywhere you went, everywhere you looked, you could witness people having the most important day of their lives: the day for which all other days had been a preparation. In the midst of the Games, unrolling and unfolding before me, I understood at last what the Games were all about.

The final of the men's 100 metres took place on Saturday. It was to start at noon, an hour chosen with the prime-time of the eastern United States firmly in mind. It was an unforgiving day, the sun striking down like a hammer, the flashbulb light that never for one instant blinked. I resolved to go, in the belief that such experiences were good for a fledgling sportswriter. I had not been asked to write about the race for Monday's paper, but I thought there might be times when I would write about this race in the future. It was one of the defining experiences of my sporting life.

I remember the glowing red of the track. I remember meeting my old friend, the sportswriter Pete Nicholls. "Lewis," I said. "Carl Lewis, for me." "Nah," said Pete. "Johnson'll win if he doesn't break down."

Ben Johnson. The Canadian sprinter who had trailed behind Lewis for some years – and then improved dramatically. He won a bronze behind Lewis at the Olympic Games in L.A. in 1984, failed to make the semis in the World Championships the following year, but in 1987, he broke the world record, 9.83 seconds. Then, in February 1988, he injured a hamstring, and injured it again in May. One chance. Had he already missed it? He was, Pete believed, ready either to win or to fall apart in trying. Lewis had other ideas. "The gold medal is mine," he said at his presser. Not a man given either to humility or public relations.

Lewis wrote about the start in his autobiography *Inside Track*: "Ben looked like a weight-lifter, and I was used to that by now, but those yellow eyes… I couldn't stop thinking about those yellow eyes. The bastard did it again, I said to myself."

The red track, the red vest of Johnson, the light that hurt. The long, fraught, gunslinger wait. The starter's gun.

Bang.

And it was over. Johnson broke from the blocks like the bullet the gun had fired. He looked like a human bullet, with his shaved head, his body pared down for action like a destroyer. He started with eye-baffling speed and the race was settled in those first two or three strides. The battle for second place went on somewhere behind him as, like the echo from his own explosion, he reached the finish. He went so fast I couldn't believe the human body could possibly take the strain: absurdly, it seemed to me that at any second, bits of him might come flying off, an arm here, a leg there. Johnson's run, I thought, exceeded the stress the human body was designed to take by a dangerous margin.

And then the final two floating strides: Johnson thrust a mighty muscled arm above his head and with a single index finger poked the sky as if to do it injury. Olympic champion. We knew we had seen something utterly remarkable even before the time flashed up on the board. But then it came: 9.79 seconds: a new world record: a new digit: a staggering seven to gaze at: four hundredths of a second better than his last record. The fastest man in the world, the fastest man in history, Superman made flesh.

And there were Pete and I, two sportswriters hired to translate this spectacle into words.

"Fuck me."

"Fuck me."

"*Fuck* me."

Wagging my head as if to shake the damn thing off my shoulders.

I decided to go to the medal-winners' press conference, and a right old wait that was too, in an uncomfortable and sweaty spot improvised at the last moment somewhere under the stands. They hadn't expected so many people. I remember some of my colleagues giving up in disgruntlement to go and seek lunch. But for some reason I stayed on. It turned out that Johnson was late, not because of arrogance, but because it had taken him an age to summon up a urine sample. He drank a couple of beers, but even so, it was a fair while in coming, Eventually he appeared: a strangely diminished person from the great warrior we had seen so recently. He was hunched and defensive, suspecting a grenade in every question, lacking confidence in his power over words, swerving questions, giving sparse answers, seeking relief in the bleeding obvious. "What means more to you, Ben – the gold medal or the world record?"

Unhesitatingly. "The gold medal. It's something nobody can ever take away."

So it was back to the hockey for me, and for various other chunks of Olympic duty. At night, back to the Media Village: here, six *Times* writers shared a floor, a common room around which six small bedrooms were grouped. Even so, there was not much privacy. When the phone went, it might have been in my own room.

It wasn't, though. The summons, at three in the morning, was for my colleague John Goodbody. John concentrated on sports news, and was then at the height of his considerable powers. This was his moment, his Olympics, the night for which all others had been a preparation. Johnson had failed a drug test, and was disqualified. Those yellow eyes, a sign of steroid use. The bastard did it all right. Get telephoning, get writing.

And I had to come to terms with the fact that one of the most amazing sporting experiences of my life was a sham.

That Johnson the hero had, in one night-shattering ringing of a telephone, metamorphosed into Johnson the villain.

But I also had to come to terms with the fact that it was still the most amazing piece of sport I had ever seen. It was still a colossal achievement. It was still an extraordinary example of self-sacrifice. We praise a man who puts his heart into his tilt at greatness. Johnson did that all right, but he also staked his liver, an organ damaged by steroids. Johnson was only giving the world what it wanted. We have an insatiable appetite for heroes: Johnson was meeting the demand as best he could. There was something genuinely heroic in that, remembering that many of the great heroes of mythology and literature destroy themselves. Johnson is perhaps sport's finest example of the self-destroying hero: sport's Oedipus.

There was an element of victimhood in Johnson's success as well as in his failure. He was being the person everybody – his country, his sport, his coach, sports followers across the world – wanted him to be. It was as if he didn't have a self: instead, he was ready to be whatever we wanted.

A year later I went to the Dubin Inquiry in Toronto, Canada's post-Johnson breast-beating. It was an examination of the Johnson case, the steroids culture and the role of Charlie Francis, Johnson's coach. There were 122 witnesses in 91 days. I was there for the opening, and Johnson's evidence. It was dismayingly frank: alarmingly innocent. As if Johnson had never thought about the matter long enough to wonder if what he was doing was either morally wrong or physically dangerous. Steroids? Human growth hormone? "If Charlie gave 'em to me, I took 'em."

Thus Johnson became the greatest villain in sport, the

man who betrayed us all. It helped that he was black, I think, and that most of the wailers and hand-wringers were white. But more than that, it seems to me that there was an over-whelming desire to punish Johnson for our own too-great faith: for our own too-great love of sport. It was this love of ours that inspired Johnson to take the drugs to improve his performance. Because we didn't want to see a man doing his best: we wanted to see a man at the far edge of the poss-ible, amazing us with things we never thought a human be-ing could do. Johnson obliged. In order to do so, he had to become superhuman – and at the same time less than human. This willingness to take that step was the thing that dismayed us most.

Sport does strange things to people, those who watch it, those who write about it, those who do it. It pushes us all into warped and distorted views of life, and sometimes into warped and distorted action. First we want heroes, then we want superheroes. Johnson obliged, in the only way he could.

29. Joe Montana

ONE OF THE REASONS we travel is to have the most homely truths confirmed. The most banal maxim acquires a vigour it never had before when encountered in French; the ordinary behaviour of people encountered in unfamiliar places comes as a shattering revelation. We travel to seek the exotic: we find the universal. We could find the same lessons at home, but they take on a new vividness when we find them on our travels.

I had already found sporting heroism in Streatham, in Birmingham, in Leeds, in the London postal district of SW19. Now I was a travelling man looking for sporting heroes further afield, hoping to find them in exotic locations and outlandish clothes. And I was delighted by the differences but more deeply affected by the similarities.

It was mostly in the United States that I went looking for different sport and different heroes, unfamiliar-looking heroes who displayed the same old heroism. I developed a mad passion for the place as I savoured my metamorphosis into travelling sportswriter. It was a great adventure, radically different from my previous peregrinations around Asia. For a start, I had some kind of status, in a place where such things matter. I had a nice hotel, a valid American Express card and an enviable job. "You go watch sports?" the taxi- drivers would ask. "And you get paid?"

So I swaggered and postured my way across the continent, visiting great sporting events, drinking Wild Turkey and fancying myself no end of a fellow. In 1987, I was one of the first three or four English sportswriters to cover the Super Bowl, the grand finale of the American football season. I went on to cover three more Super Bowls, two World Series and I watched Michael Jordan winning the NBA championship with the Chicago Bulls.

One afternoon sums it all up. One hero captures that adventure for all time. Here, in a foreign land, in a strange type of fancy dress, playing a game filled with complex and esoteric rules, accompanied by a weird culture and a glorious, exotic language, was a man who found the greatest of himself at the time of the greatest need. As every sports hero should. His name was Joe Montana; he was quarterback for the San Francisco 49ers.

As the 49ers went into the Super Bowl of 1989 – Super Bowl XXIII, if you like – against the brilliant upstarts, the Cincinnati Bengals, Montana was 32. People had been suggesting he had lost his nerve. That's a big thing for any athlete, but especially so for a quarterback. His job is to be a living target. He must wait, wait until the man is free and he can throw his pass. Wait and risk getting flattened, flattened often in a peculiarly disquieting way, by someone you simply haven't seen. You must look for men to pass to, not for enemies about to scrag you. Some suggested that Montana no longer had what it took to wait: that he was throwing passes too quickly. Fear had conquered him. In the course of the season he had had a row with the 49ers coach, Bill Walsh, and had lost his place to the back-up quarterback, Steve Young, before winning it back again. The 49ers reached the Super Bowl after travelling to play a tumultuous game against the Chicago Bears, on as cold a day as I have ever experienced in my life. There were reheating stations at each corner of the stadium, and notices telling you what to do should your companion's skin colour alter dramatically. These were Chicago conditions, Bear weather, but the San Francisco side triumphed. No doubt they remembered Mark Twain's remark "the coldest winter I ever spent was a summer in San Francisco".

On, then, to Miami and the Super Bowl. The occasion began with race riots and zoned-off areas and sportswriters pretending to be hard news reporters and sending home stuff about tension walking the streets of strife-torn Miami. The Bengals, with their sassy young quarterback Boomer Esiason – not, I think, his baptismal name – were strongly favoured in some quarters to change the balance of power in the sport, and they took what looked like a decisive lead with just a few minutes to go. I had bet on the 49ers with Simon Kellner, a colleague from the *Independent* who went on to become the paper's editor. He favoured the Bengals. Boomer was his man, and he was celebrating as the Bengals took their narrow lead and the 49ers were faced with an impossible 92 yards to gain with three minutes and ten seconds left on the clock. I remember shouting at Kellner in the din: "It's not over! Look at that guy! Look at that guy!"

That guy was Montana, walking into the huddle. I could see, even from the dizzy height of the press box, that every line of his body was that of a man of purpose. One of his team was to say afterwards that Montana walked into the huddle like John Wayne. In normal life, at normal times, Montana was an insignificant-looking fellow, strangely unimpressive for a man of his size, a great spouter of press conference clichés, a bland and forgettable face. But there he was, clad in his shoulder pads, his helmet, the grill over his face, the number 16 on his back. And he took on himself the aspect of a hero.

So it began. I knew the rules, all about first and ten, unnecessary roughness, facemask holding and the declining of penalties. I was familiar with the game's rhythms and even to an extent with its tactics. And I knew that the task of driving his team forward 92 yards was not on. As impossible as England winning a Test match after following on against Australia.

Montana started to throw. Not great hit-and-hope, shit-or-bust passes, the type of pass American football people charmingly call a Hail Mary. These were sharp, often short, methodical, incisive, purposeful. He went time and again to his favourite men, Jerry Rice and Roger Craig. Then a penalty forced the play back, back ten yards, enough to kill any last remaining hopes the 49ers had.

That's when Montana stepped things up. He threw to Rice, who made a stretching, beautiful catch for 27 yards. On they went, advancing play by play across the griddle of the pitch. By this time the noise in the stadium was pop concert loud, jet take-off loud. Montana had to call each play five times to make sure everybody heard. He shouted so loudly, out of necessity, that he began hyperventilating. His head span, he grew dizzy, he signalled to his coach Walsh for a time-out. Walsh, unaware of his plight, eager to keep up the momentum, turned him down.

There was a point when the 49ers could have gone for a tying field goal, but they went for the lot instead. The last play was 20 Halfback Curl X Up. Craig went one way, Rice, the key man, another. Montana minced back seven paces as a quarterback does, eyes busy. And then he hurled the pointed ball like a javelin, and it went straight into the heart of the endzone, straight at the heart of John Taylor, who had run and jinked his way to a spot just in front of the solitary post that supported the goal. Victory. Quite impossibly, victory for the 49ers, victory for Montana, victory for the universal qualities that heroes possess.

Montana had kept his head while all around were losing theirs. But it was not just calmness that Montana found in these climactic minutes: it was the ability to play better than he had ever played before. And that really is the essence of great sport: to find your best when you need it most. I've seen that in London and Beijing, in Miami and Yokohama, in Manchester and Adelaide and Merthyr Tydfil. It is one of sport's universal truths. You can find it in a man in muddy shorts in an industrial town in the north of England, in a woman in a white dress in south London, and as now, in a man wearing gold trousers and a shining golden helmet. "Everything that was necessary for his team to win the football game today, Montana did," said Boomer. "We were just 34 seconds away from a great victory. The next thing you know you're using all the losing clichés you can."

Montana said it was "really sweet".

30. Ayrton Senna

THERE ARE SOME GREAT performers in sport who pride themselves on their ordinariness. They cope with the extraordinary demands they make on themselves by pretending to be just like everybody else. Others prefer to be one of the crowd, only more so: one of the lads, but ever-so-slightly more laddish, men who like to be earthy and companionable and just that little bit more successful with women, that little bit more able to hold their drink. There are some, more women than men, who cope by concentrating on their weaknesses, on their pressing need to improve, to work harder. It is rare to find a great performer in sport who believes in his uniqueness, his complete singularity of nature, his specialness, his separation from the normal run of humankind.

But Ayrton Senna was like that. I learned this during a haunting encounter standing in the sun in Montreal. I was making a complicated journey around Canada and the United States, a trip that included my day at the Dubin Inquiry in Toronto to hear the evidence of Ben Johnson. I travelled, by way of New York State, to Montreal, for the Grand Prix, and after assiduous telephoning, I won the considerable prize of an interview with Senna.

I was early, he was late. But at least I could see him. He was standing up in the McLaren motorhome, talking to the team boss, Ron Dennis. Talking, talking. I could see through the window his intense face, his two fists every so often flying up to his face as he clutched a steering wheel of air. It seemed he would never emerge, but at last he came out and joined me in the sun. I asked him a first question. I can't remember how it went, something easy, some kind of warm-up question.

There was a long silence. I was about to break it, try another shot, when something stopped me. I suddenly realised that Senna was translating my question into Portuguese, running it through, thinking of an answer and translating that answer into English. I was aware, even before he had given me an answer, that he was a strange, aloof person but not one who automatically despised other people. I have met many who plume their egos by being insolent to the press people they have in their power. Senna wasn't remotely interested in that, being, for a start, too secure in his sense of self. Besides, it was clear before he opened his mouth that he was a man who, when he did anything, would do it to the best of his ability. Even in the banal circumstances of a press interview, he was a man without compromise.

"I still don't know how far I can go. It is all a learning process, something I work very hard to keep clear in my mind. I aim to have a realistic, clear understanding of what is going on, and what I am doing – and what I can do. I can only try what I believe I can do, but trying, I often find I can do more. Then I have to readjust."

It was in this constant readjustment of limits that Senna began to wonder if he had any limits at all. If he had, they were certainly different from other people's limits. He was a man of extraordinary talent, and an extraordinary view of himself.

"On many occasions I have gained more satisfaction from beating my own achievements. Many times I find myself in a comfortable position – and I don't feel happy about it. I feel it is right to slow down, but something inside of me, something very strong, pushes me on, makes me try to beat myself. It is… an enormous desire to go further and further to travel beyond my own limits – but when I establish limits that are higher than anyone else's, then I want to beat them. I want to beat myself.

"Every time I have an idea about where my limits are, I go to check it and most of the time I am wrong. So I have to adjust myself to going even further. It is very exciting, and it is a non-stop process. You set a record, like for pole position, and OK, it is gone. So I have to do something else, another step."

It was a strange encounter. This man didn't seem quite part of the world. He was unlike anyone else I had ever interviewed. There was something rather spooky about it all, and it stayed with me. So much so that I began to pay more attention to the strange world of Formula One. Senna's success became deeply important to me. His mad quest for perfection had made the whole bizarre circus tremendously vivid. Senna made a glorious contrast with his rival and sometimes teammate, Alain Prost, a man who shied away from limits, whose measured, pragmatic racing always took place with a little bit to spare. Always, he had control. He was known as "the Professor", a strange nickname for a racing driver. He and Senna were involved in a number of shocking and rather shaming incidents. Senna frequently believed himself victimised, especially by the autocratic head of the international federation, the absurd Jean-Marie Balestre.

Senna went on to win three World Driver's titles. He was a phenomenon. Formula One is a sport that should only take place in rain, when the advantage of car and engine is nullified, and a race becomes a true test of the skill and courage of the human pilots. Senna was the best – best of all time – in the rain, finding grip – and daring to seek it – in circumstances where anyone else would either back off or spin off. He really was every bit as good as he believed he was. Or very nearly.

Because he died. He was killed on the racetrack. He was killed at Monza in Italy in the third race of the season of 1994, in a Williams car that had a number of serious problems. It was strange, cursed weekend: Roland Ratzenburger had been killed the previous day in qualifying. There was a feeling of doom as the race day began. But I still didn't think that it would be Senna. I still remember my response when I had the call from *The Times*: we think Senna is dead, can you stand by to write? Stupidly, I couldn't believe that Senna, Senna of all people, would die. Not like that. I had, it seemed, been taken in by Senna's own view of the world and his place in it. I had believed that for some men, life really is different. That they really do operate under different rules. That Senna really was a hero, a favourite of the gods. I should have remembered that heroes who are favoured by one god often incur the enmity of another.

"Power comes from my education, which you would say was privileged," Senna told me on that Montreal afternoon. "I was privileged to grow up in a happy and healthy environment. I had my family always behind me, helping me when I have some doubt, some question… and on top of that, I have been able to experience God's power on earth."

Some people have talked of a death wish, others of a man rendered dangerous by his belief in his own uniqueness.

Senna was a man of blazing intensity and unshakeable

belief. Religion is used as a sporting metaphor nearly as often as war: a stadium becomes a cathedral, fans are the faithful, new managers are messiahs, and on and on. In some ways, sport does seek to fill the void religion left. But sport doesn't pass muster, in that it has no core belief, no faith, and a somewhat ambiguous relationship with moral codes. But it does fulfil some of the old functions of religion. Religion has many tales of great people and noble deeds, and many fables and parables to make important moral points. Religion is full of the lives of the saints, a litany of heroes, a panheroikon for the faith, many of whom gave up their lives for what they believed in. Senna was the sort of person who, in an earlier age, would have been a saint. A martyr, obviously. There was always something deeply dangerous about Senna, but in the end, he was the one in danger. I think now that I was aware of this without knowing it, after our only meeting. That was why I felt strangely protective of him during his brilliant and turbulent career. That's why my first reaction on hearing of his death was disbelief. I had known all along that men like Senna are headed somewhere terrible, but I preferred not to understand that. I preferred Senna's own evaluation of the world.

There is one Senna story I always remember. Senna was being rebuked for some minor motor-racing sin, some error of protocol, some disregarding of convention. It was in genuine bafflement that he pointed out: "But I am Senna."

1990s

31. Steffi Graf

STEFFI GRAF STARTED PLAYING tennis when she was three, and started playing in tournaments when she was five. This isn't so terribly unusual. Many champions, especially in tennis, start frighteningly early. But so do an awful lot of people who never became champions. I can never read of a champion's oppressed early life without thinking about all those early starters who weren't good enough, all those children nurtured as champions who never got to the top, all those turtles who never reached the sea. How do they survive in the real world, when they have to make a start without the benefit of a childhood? How does the relationship with the disappointed parent work out? How does it affect the rest of their lives, what they do for a living, who they share that life with?

Graf was reared to be a champion by her mad and intense father Peter, who had worked as a tennis coach. She turned professional in 1982, and had her first full year as a pro the following year. By then, she was 13. She was fiercely protected. Her life was based around practice, four hours a day. Her father had complete control of such social life as she had. Cannily, he didn't put her into too many tournaments, going for long-term rather than short-term glory. And money.

As a result, Graf slowly eased into the world's awareness as a talented but unknowable teenager. She was a shy person who had been given no chance to be anything else. Most public appearances – those when she had to speak rather than wield a racket – were a torment to her. She hid behind muttered clichés and a sheepdog haircut. I remember the great sports photographer Eamonn McCabe telling me how hard it was to get a decent photograph of her: great action, but no face. You couldn't see who was lurking behind that flopping hair, that eyebrow-length fringe. She gave nothing away in interviews or press conferences. She gave the impression of aloofness, of not really caring much about the rest of the world. She was a person who alienated sympathy. No one made much allowance for her years, for her upbringing, but that's sport for you. If you are old enough to compete at the top level, you are old enough to be judged. It's your choice.

She was all forehand, and it was already a fearsome weapon. She favoured it any time the shot was possible: a great, belabouring inside-out take-that-you-hound sort of blow. On the backhand she favoured the slice, and could cut people to ribbons with it: accurate, long, and hanging infuriatingly in the air. And she could serve at up to 110 mph.

By 1986, the year she turned 15, she was beating top play-ers like Chris Evert and Martina Navratilova; the following year she beat Navratilova to win the French Open. She had arrived all right. The following year she won the lot – all four grand-slam singles titles, plus a gold medal at the Olympic Games in Seoul: the Golden Slam, they called it. In the final of the French, she beat Natasha Zvereva 6-0, 6-0, a double-bagel in 32 minutes, She lost only 13 points. She won Wim-bledon after going a set and a two-love down to Navratilova, losing only one more game of the next 13.

One of the drawbacks of being a precocious athlete, or for that matter, a member of the royal family, is that you have to do your growing up in public. You have to have a public adolescence. Boris Becker, who won Wimbledon at 17 and was something of a spoiled intellectual, was forever thinking out loud in press conferences, rather endearingly on the whole. Graf was never one to give herself away in these circumstances. I remember my old friend, the former tennis correspondent of *The Times*, Rex Bellamy, being the first journalist on record to be rewarded that brilliance of Graf's smile. He asked her – she must have been 14 at the time – if she had a dog. She did: she was a doggy person, like Rex, and the room and most of the surrounding area lit up with her response.

But mostly, she was regarded as a person who possessed talent and very little else. No personality. And as for personal appearance, well, a plain old thing: a nose not unlike Concorde occasionally visible between the hangar-roof of a fringe and two great walls of blonde hair.

And then one day she was beautiful. She tied her hair back from her face. At times of relaxation, she would smile. Suddenly, she was a woman in full possession of herself: suddenly, it was legitimate to admire the way she looked. The power and grace she played with lost any of its previous awkwardness. And it is in the astonishing, almost overnight metamorphosis that Graf established her heroic credentials. She had made the extraordinary transition that all of us must make, in some way or another, from being an adolescent to being a grown-up. We all must also make that other transition, from being somebody else's person to being our own person, but Graf had more need of doing that than most. And she did so while losing none of her force. In some ways, she was more forceful than before: she was no longer doing it to please another. She could walk away whenever she wished.

Graf's complex relationship with her father is the story of most of her life. There were problems other than the obvious ones here. There was talk of her father's extra-marital affairs; when she was questioned about them at Wimbledon in 1990, she broke down in tears. Later there were problems with money and unpaid taxes dating back to those very early years: Peter was sentenced to 45 months in prison and served 25 of them; Steffi later paid DM1.3 million.

But somewhere along the line some kind of weaning took place. The best and most revealing story about tennis parents can be found in André Agassi's book, *Open*. Agassi was to marry Graf, and the fathers had to meet. Both were impossible, maniacal, bullying tennis parents who had each made a tennis champion. Both these champions then made a dramatic transition from adolescent to grown-up, Graf by tying her hair back, Agassi by shaving off what was left of his hair and abandoning his "frosted mullet" hairpiece. The two tennis fathers first argued about backhands, and then about who would beat whom if it came to boxing. Graf's father was then 63, Agassi's 61. "Pete is trash-talking in German, my father is trash-talking in Assyrian, and they're both putting up their fists. They're circling, feinting, bobbing and weaving, and just before one of them throws hands, I step in, push them apart." André went home to his Stefanie. "I don't know when a margarita has ever tasted so good."

Graf survived her childhood, and her father's interventions in her later life. And as she did so, she picked up 22 grand-slam singles titles, winning all four titles at least four times. She was number one for 377 weeks, and year-end number one eight times. She won the first few prizes because she was told to and the rest because she chose to. She did so with style and grace and beauty. She retired in 1999, married Agassi two years later and they have two children, neither of whom is forced to play tennis.

32. Eric Cantona

THE NOTION OF WHAT makes a hero shifts and changes and contradicts itself throughout our lives. At a certain age, we begin to accept the idea that a hero can still be a hero while showing himself less perfect than we had hoped, more flawed that we had suspected. As we move on still further, we can accept that a hero's private life may be a matter of disaster and horror. Further on again, we can accept that some heroes have their being in error and folly: that we can find little or no excuse for them and what they do – while at the same time, their stories somehow matter to us. But perhaps the final frontier is absurdity. There comes a point when we can see a person who is in some ways utterly ridiculous, and yet still commands the role of hero. We can take the ridiculousness in our stride, perhaps even revel in it.

"I wanted to act even when I was still playing football." So said Eric Cantona. And act he did. He was the biggest ham actor that ever stepped across the touchline. He overplayed the part of himself to a ludicrous degree, walking with his shoulder-blades touching, his collar turned up, his feet smearing insects at every step. It was that walk that made Manchester United what it is today, made the Premier League what it is, made the football industry what it is.

Why did he come to England? Because his psychiatrist recommended it. He was a Frenchman; he spent his early years, apparently, in a cave in Marseilles. He played for any number of French clubs, and he was banned or at least suspended by most of them, generally for picking fights with team-mates. There's scarcely a club he played for where he didn't have a fight with someone. Opponents got off comparatively lightly, but everyone who thwarted him was fair game. After one incident in a match, when he threw the ball at the ref and was sent off, he was disciplined and banned for a month. His response was to stand in front on each member of the judging panel in turn and scream at him the same word: *"Idiot!"* For some reason, his ban was doubled.

Perhaps his psychiatrist thought that if he didn't speak the language, he would find fewer reasons to hit people. Anyway, he played 15 games for Leeds United in 1991, enough to make them the last champions before the Premier League began. The following season, Manchester United were having trouble scoring goals. Sir Alec Ferguson, the Manchester United manager, was involved in a long and complex phone call with Leeds United. Almost as an afterthought, he asked about Cantona's availability. He acquired him for £1.2 million. It was probably the best value-for-money transfer in history, even in purely footballing terms.

With Cantona, Manchester United changed almost overnight. Perhaps it is better to say that with Cantona, they at last became themselves. They had, after all, pretty well everything they needed already. The only thing missing was a sense of self: a sense of being better than everyone else, a sense of being privileged, a sense of being special. This Cantona was able to provide in lavish quantities. It showed in his spectacular skills in training, in his attitude, in his swagger, in the way he expected opponents to curl up and die for him. Cantona made goals and scored them, and did so with a crushing and overwhelming presence. He scored brilliant, unorthodox goals: he opened up avenues to goal, often with a backheel which, as a lover of paradox, was his signature trick.

He wasn't a great player in the way that Pele, Johan Cruyff or Franz Beckenbauer were. He was a man who preferred to dominate the smaller stages. He was never a great footballer, in the loftiest understanding of the term. Rather, he was a great footballing catalyst. He was the great enabler. The season he joined, Manchester United won their first championship since 1967. They have been reeling them off ever since. Cantona was with them for five years; in that time they won the league title four times, with two league and FA Cup doubles. Under Cantona, Manchester United became the natural champions of England. The same sense of entitlement shines through today. Thanks to Cantona, every Manchester United team that has ever lined up for any competition has done so with the insolence of champions.

Cantona played the part of the stage French intellectual. He liked to behave as if he spent most of his time in pavement cafés, discussing existentialism for hours at a time over a single *petit noir*, between occasional bouts of playing football, with Albert Camus presumably the goalkeeper. He talked about the ball "responding to my caresses like a woman with the man she loved". He was superior to everyone. Mind you, you get the impression that if every footballer had been well-read and prone to gnomic utterances and intellectual references, Cantona would have played the ignorant thug. There's a song by The Kinks: "I'm not like everybody else".

An egomaniac of Cantona's class needs to be in a team. This is not to curb his excesses but to showcase them. You can't be a paradox or an exception on your own: you have a terrible need for ordinary people. Cantona imposed his fantasy of entitlement on the sporting world around him, and amazingly often, he found himself indulged. His desire for personal remarkability seemed to compel obedience. But at the same time, there were problems when things like reality got in Cantona's way. He berated referees and got sent off, he assaulted opponents and got sent off. In 1994, he was sent off two matches in succession. I was there for the first of these: a cultured backheel into a fallen opponent.

His most famous excess was his assault on a supporter. He was sent off at Crystal Palace and was making his way around the touchline towards the changing rooms to a chorus of insults, when it became too much. He launched a flying kick at the throat of a supporter – yes, there were plenty of shit-hits-the-fan jokes – and was arrested. The supporter in question, Matthew Simmons, turned out to have a criminal record and form as a supporter of the National Front. He was charged with threatening behaviour and language and was given a fine. My old friend Richard Williams of the *Guardian* wrote that the only thing Cantona did wrong "was to stop kicking him".

Cantona was initially sentenced to two weeks in prison, later changed on appeal to 120 hours' community service. He gave a brief address to the press afterwards: "When seagulls follow the trawler, it is because they think sardines will be thrown into the sea." After this not really terribly enigmatic remark, he said no more. Hamming it up to the end.

He served his long suspension from the game, came back, resumed his place with Manchester United and found more glory, though success on the still larger stage of European competition was beyond both him and his club at the time. He was able to take them only so far, though his legacy remains. He retired not far beyond his peak, strutting off to do his acting thing.

One of the great tragedies of Cantona's life was that he was not quite as good as he wanted to be, as he believed himself to be. His real worth did not add up to his own assessment of it. To maintain his personal myth, Cantona needed to be better than he really was. His uncontrollable violence was an expression of that disappointment, those terrible moments when he could see the rift between fantasy and reality. And in truth, he wasn't really as clever as he wanted to be either. He was by footballing standards a great intellectual, much as Camus was, by the standards of intellectuals, a great goalkeeper.

But he still transformed football and gave it that sense of self-worth it has today. Perhaps that's not entirely – or even at all – a good thing. Nevertheless, his time in England was vivid, unforgettable and every bit as glorious as it was ludicrous. "I have had a lot of good moments," he summed up. "But the one I prefer is when I kicked the hooligan."

33. Florence Griffith-Joyner

HARD TO GET MORE absurd than Florence Griffith-Joyner. But when we met, there was a wholly unexpected touch of pathos about her. Against all logic, I felt an odd pity for her. The year was 1989; the previous year she had performed with sumptuous brilliance at the Olympic Games, winning three gold medals. With her flashy looks and her blistering speed, she was an instant global darling. Flo-Jo had conquered the world. And yet there was something I couldn't place about her: vulnerability, shyness, perhaps disappointment, perhaps even shame.

It began with an iridescent mauve body suit. Flashy, but not flashy enough for Griffith-Joyner. She added a pair of blue-and-white knickers. Still not enough. So she cut away one leg, to give herself an appearance of extraordinary exoticism. She wore this outfit at the United States Olympic Trials: she ran the 100 metres in 10.49 seconds. This was a world record. It is still a world record. No one else is even close.

She went to the Olympic Games in Seoul in 1988 and was uncatchable. She won the 100 metres in 10.54, her smile exploding onto her face with 20 metres still to go. She then won the 200 metres in 21.34. That record still stands as well. She won gold in the 4x100 metres relay, and then, astonishingly, won silver in the 4x400, showing an almost unprecedented virtuosity.

This was the Olympic Games of Ben Johnson: the ending of the age of innocence, the final demolition of trust between athletes and spectators. And everything about Griffith-Joyner suggested the classic pattern for the use of anabolic steroids and human growth hormone: the sudden impossibly steep improvement, the equally sudden dramatic change in body shape, the muscles, the prognathous jaw, the deepening voice. Yet she never failed a drug test. She retired with devastating suddenness, a year or so after we met. That was shortly after they introduced out-of-competition drug-testing. All these significant things, all these nudges, all those winks. And not a shred of hard evidence.

We met at the Four Seasons Hotel in Orange County, north of Los Angeles. She wore a tracksuit that must have taken 30 seconds to choose and put on, and make-up that must have taken hours. She was an hour late, giving me a terrible fear that I had spent a great deal of money on flights and two nights at the Four Seasons for a no-show. But she showed: made an entrance rather, striding across the lobby as if she knew all the world would recognise her, and as if she was slightly worried that it might not.

So I asked her about drugs. "We all know you're on some-thing, Florence," I said, for we became matey fairly briskly. It's an ugly name in an American mouth: "Flawrnts". I gave it a cute-British-accent disyllabic validity. "What was it, Flor-ence? Essence of panther?"

She lowered her eyes shyly: "Oh no, Simon. I just gave it my ahhhhllllll." It was a lovely voice, whispering, and with just that hint of the bass-baritone to keep you alarmed. And she gave as perfect a performance of American aspiration culture as you could wish for. Doing your nails, designing clothes, writing a children's book – it all came down to giving your ahhhhllll. "When children say I want to be just like you, I say, don't say that. You want to be yourself, as great as you can be."

Being the fastest wasn't enough for Griffith-Joyner. She had to draw all eyes upon her. Becoming a champion was the way to become a star. Without her talent for running, she would have been a star in the local shopping mall.

A vignette. We got into the lift together, because we borrowed a hotel room for an hour. We were accompanied by a photographer and her husband: we were going to do a photo-shoot, what else? "What floor?" she asked. Top, what else? And so she *knuckled* the lift button. She couldn't touch it with her fingertip like a normal human being because her nails were an inch long, maybe more. You could see her on the blocks at the start of the race, every competitor but her resting on fingertips, Griffith-Joyner on her knuckles. And I thought then: how many tasks, both public and private, is she unable to perform because of this crippling affectation? How much work does it take to maintain it? How many things, from making love to eating a plate of spaghetti, are compromised?

It wasn't even attractive. Those nails, painted bright pink, had taken on odd, twisted shapes as they grew, writhing in the manner of trees on a wind-blasted slope. There was something eerie about those nails, something that spoke of bottomless reserves of self-obsession. She held them nonchalantly in view for the camera and smiled her sunburst smile.

Nine years later she was dead. She was 38. There were great whoops of glee in certain quarters. It was a morality tale, they crowed, and she had been justly punished for her use of drugs. But drugs had nothing to do with her death. It wasn't something she had taken: it was something she was born with. She had an epileptic fit and suffocated on her pillow.

As to drugs, nothing was proved either way at the post-mortem. Presumably she did use drugs: after all, we have those unbeatable times in the record books. They are the stand-out examples of a number of embarrassing super-fast times that are still unbeaten, reminders of the darkest days of track and field.

There was an ineffable silliness about Griffith-Joyner. There was also a sense of something missing. It was as if she had built herself, piece by piece, into a star: the clothes, the aspirational philosophy, the make-up, the nails, the body, the speed – every item manufactured and put in place by her own hand.

And I had the terrible feeling that it wasn't enough. She had done everything that anyone could, in order to be everything that everybody could possibly want her to be. She was fast, successful, glamorous, full of good ol' American optimism, a self-help book on two shapely hyper-swift legs, one of them clad in lycra, the other naked. What more could anyone want? What more, indeed, could anyone give?

But there was something about her that wasn't quite right. I couldn't ever quite forget it: that sense of pathos, that feeling of a lost, a damaged person. "Be cool and follow your dream," she told me. She had followed hers: and I suspect that something in her found it wanting. Either the dream, or the method of attaining it. Or even both.

There was something of Janis Joplin in her: Joplin who said: "I love being a star more than life itself." In some ways, Florence Griffith-Joyner is just another rock-and-roll casualty. But at least we still have her records.

She makes it into these pages as a hero because her story

has haunted me: her silly persona, her clichés, her awkward-ness, her desire to please, her ultimate failure to do so. There are tragic elements to her story. When you give your all, you don't have a great deal left to call your own.

34. Mike Atherton

AS I'VE SAID BEFORE, you're not supposed to meet your heroes. Well, I've met Mike Atherton. I've sat next to the bugger for days at a time. I've dined with him, I've had beers with him. Atherton was an exceptional cricketer; he is now a television commentator with *Sky* and chief cricket correspondent for *The Times*, and since in most press boxes writers from the same paper have adjacent seats, I have had plenty of time to be disillusioned, or not, on the subject of Atherton and his heroism.

Well, since he is included here, you'll see I haven't been disillusioned, but that is probably because I wasn't terribly il-lusioned in the first place. It wasn't a problem establishing the cheerful, knockabout, rough-and-ready bantering, favour-swapping relationship that exists between good colleagues: something more than a strictly business relationship, though not quite a friendship in the ordinary sense of the term. It's an intimacy of an altogether different kind.

Atherton is a man who carries no side whatsoever, which makes things a lot easier. But that's true of most of the pro-fessional cricketers who become written-press journos. They have to come into the press box and learn a new trade in front of a bunch of people who are long accustomed to the craft of writing to a deadline. This acquisition of a second skill is demanding and occasionally humbling. They have, at least up to a point, to reinvent themselves.

But it would be wrong to say that Atherton's cricketing past plays no part in the relationship he has with me, or with everybody else in a professional and cricketing context. You can't help but be aware of it. It is part of him; it can't be any-thing else. If his cricket was an expression of his nature, then that nature still existed long after the cricket had gone. We were talking books, not for the first time, and I was trying to talk Atherton into reading *Ulysses*. I started laughing: "It's not as if I have to teach you about not giving up."

On another occasion, we were having a drink at a bar. Or rather we weren't, because I was trying to buy them and I had, as usual, donned my cloak of invisibility before stepping up and waving banknotes at an uninterested barman. Eventually I caught his reluctant attention, and he served the drinks. Atherton then leant over the bar. In a quiet, conversational tone he said: "You ignored my friend while he was standing at the bar, even though you weren't busy. That is appallingly unprofessional. Don't let it happen again." He then turned to me and raised his glass and resumed the conversation. Leaving me quietly staggered. We were in Australia, the barman had no idea who was talking to him. But Atherton's startling self-confidence, his willingness to take on anybody that he thought needed taking on, was remarkable. I could have said the same things myself, of course, but not without getting angry and making a scene. It was the ease of manner that was so devastating. It certainly devastated the hell out of the barman. When Atherton bought the next round the man was practically standing to attention, and Australians don't normally go in for subservience.

Atherton's entire career was a battle against ineptitude. During the 1990s, his was the one wicket that mattered. In a dismal period for English cricket, Atherton was the only man you could rely on. He scored runs, but when he was out, it generally happened that everyone else was out soon after. He got used to standing alone: the boy on the burning deck of

English cricket. He was made captain at the age of 25 and held the job for five years: five years in which he was mostly trying to stave off defeat. He knew, and the opposition knew, that once he was gone, the rest would probably follow.

But quite often, he wasn't gone. Quite often, he was able to face down the opposition and fight back. He was a man beleaguered, but beleaguerment suited him. Above all, he relished personal up-against-it combat: the duel within the battle that is at the heart of Test match cricket. In his early days, the moustached Australian bowler and buffoon Merv Hughes made a furious onslaught on the baby-faced Pommy batsman in front of him. Atherton responded with a small v-shaped smile. Sledging always made Atherton stronger.

His defining moment actually lasted more than 11 hours – one hell of a moment. It was, of course, an innings up against it. England were playing South Africa in Johannes-burg. Atherton saved the match by batting for two days for 185 runs. It was a masterpiece of stubbornness. It was like reading *Ulysses* in Afrikaans. It was a transparent effort of the will, and English cricket followers celebrated the triumph as if it was the Ashes and the World Cup combined. Cheering for England cricket was at that time a rare luxury.

My own, and most other people's most vivid memory of Atherton comes from another series against South Africa. Everything was right about it: it came on a Sunday teatime, when Test cricket was still on terrestrial television. Just about everybody with a passing interest in sport seems to have seen it. It was a passage of play at Trent Bridge. South Africa were 1-0 up in the series: England needed 247 to win. One wicket would do it, so long as it was Atherton's. Alan Donald took his second spell, and bowled frighteningly fast from round the wicket, sending a series of snorting short-pitched balls at the body. Atherton took what he couldn't avoid. Donald got him, too, caught behind off the glove, but Atherton stood his ground and the umpire turned down the appeal. Donald bowled on in a fury, firing bouncers and insults and taunts: Atherton, face still as if carved, stared unfathomably back through the grill of his helmet. England reached their target the following day, with Atherton unbeaten on 98. His failure to get a century was deeply appropriate: it was victory that mattered far more than a personal milestone.

Atherton was dismayingly frank in his excellent autobiography *Opening Up*. "At this stage, I was definitely a tough player… Physically I was fit and I have no doubt that there is a connection between physical and mental fitness. Mental toughness, however, was never a constant with me. Towards the end of my career I was definitely less strong. Like a boxer who has taken too many blows, by the end, mentally, I had had enough."

Mental toughness was Atherton's defining feature: odd to hear him decry his own lack of it. Perhaps a less mentally tough person would find it impossible to confess this weakness. Atherton assesses his own career fairly bleakly, and concludes that he was not a great cricketer, as he had hoped to be. He had an average of 38, a shade below the highest class, and was always vulnerable to Glenn McGrath, the Australian fast bowler and nonpareil; he was out to McGrath 19 times in his career, a Test match record.

But if Atherton himself denies his own claims for greatness, we must conclude that heroism doesn't necessarily require greatness. It merely requires a tale: a context in which heroic deeds can be performed. Atherton's context was the darkest and most dismal period in the history of English cricket. But there was always Atherton. The cry "Atherton's out" would cast the country into gloom, because we knew what always followed. Atherton led the fight against despair, the battle against the darkness. In the endless sequence of inevitable defeats to overwhelmingly superior opposition, Atherton gave meaning and value to the struggle.

He still hasn't finished *Ulysses*. But I don't think he's given up.

35. Frankie Dettori

PERFECTION MAY BE A rare thing in sport, but it is just about impossible in every other walk of life. We live by means of flaws: flaws remind us that we are alive and human. All great novels are flawed novels: every hero is a flawed hero: every perfect marriage has its rows and its silences and its no-go areas. Every great work of art or craft is marred as well as made by the person who created it. Islamic artists are so committed to the concept of the flaw that they will deliberately disrupt a symmetrical pattern with a carefully inserted, almost ostentatious pseudo-mistake. This is supposed to guard against presumptuousness and blasphemy, a public acknowledgement that they are not seeking to rival God, the only possible source of perfection. That strikes me as presumption in itself: a suggestion that they really would be able to rival God, if they weren't so majestically humble. Better to strive all out for perfection, in the knowledge that falling short is inevitable.

Many sports are geared for the flaws of their participants. Perfection is out of the equation right from the start. No one goes round a golf course in 18 shots. No one runs a race at the speed of light: we must all accept the limitation of the human frame, even Ben Johnson. Every moment of perfection in the confrontational sports like football and cricket is balanced by errors. Garry Sobers hit six sixes in an over: a rare example of perfection in cricket. Perfection of a kind is possible in some of the less demanding sports: the 300 game in ten-pin bowling, the nine-darter, the 147 in snooker. In snooker, the maximum possible score has such a mystique that you will see players risking defeat in a match in pursuit of the incidental goal of the perfect frame.

The impossible dream of perfection haunts us in real life: the fantasy world of sport tantalises us with its apparent possibility. Usually, little moments of perfection are followed by error: David Gower, as near perfect a batsman as ever took guard, would follow a passage of perfection with an absent-minded mistake that had the audience clasping their heads in frustration. A person who genuinely succeeds in delivering sporting perfection can't fail to be a hero: a Prometheus figure who brings us, at great personal expense, lavish gifts that we really don't deserve.

Frankie Dettori reached perfection on an afternoon in late September in 1996. This was not an ordinary race meeting: it was the Festival of British Racing at Ascot, with seven high-quality races on the card. Dettori won them all. He was ecstatic after three. The feats of the afternoon took him into a wild blur of perfection, something not unlike an out-of-body experience. As a result of this, he found a response deep within the horses that he rode.

Dettori was a greatly loved person before this extraordinary afternoon. He was that rare thing, a cheerful jockey: a jockey prepared to show the public something other than grim purpose, disciplined diet and an addiction to victory. Dettori, like Flo-Jo, loved being a star. He adored performing for his public: the big open-mouthed grins, the flying dismounts, the willingness to engage with interviewers and to give the impression that horses and racing and victory contained all the joys that life can offer.

He was – still is – a beautifully compact rider, with as good a sense of balance as I have ever seen. His father was a jockey; his mother was a circus performer who used to ride two horses at once and perform a backflip while doing so. Dettori's extreme physical control allows him to ride with his hands lower than most, a great aid in conserving the horse's effort during a race, the better to unleash it when it matters.

All kinds of riding, even that of the wham-bam nature of the jockey's trade, depend on a relationship between horse and rider, and the two-way exchange of information and emotion that operates for the duration of the partnership. As Dettori went into an ever-ascending sporting high that afternoon at Ascot, so the horses beneath him were increasingly affected by the bizarre certainty that fell on Dettori that day.

He won on Wall Street at 2-1, Diffident 12-1, Mark of Esteem 100-30, Fatefully 7-4, Decorated Hero 7-1 and Lochangel 5-4. He told the BBC interviewer Julian Wilson: "Don't touch me, because I am red-hot!" But as he got ready to ride in the last race of the day, the seventh, he told his colleague, the jockey Walter Swinburn: "I'm on a twelve or fourteen to one shot, with too much weight, who is hopelessly out of form." Swinburn told him not to worry, to go for it.

The name of the no-hoper was Fujiyama Crest. Dettori started off with extraordinary decisiveness, tracking across the course from the worst possible draw to take a position on the rails. Once there, he chose to set the pace, again an exceptionally bold decision. "In the final 100 yards Fuji was numb with exhaustion…. Somehow he conjured up a little bit more and staggered over the line." There were some cynics who thought that the jockeys gave Dettori the race, from generosity, from trade union solidarity, because they got swept up in the emotions of an extraordinary event. Dettori rejects this notion with fury. "One thing I do know for sure, if the last race had been first I wouldn't have dared be so positive on Fujiyama Crest and so he would almost certainly not have won. When you are high you have an edge, and I doubt if I'd ever been higher after winning the previous six races."

This outsider was insanely backed down to 2-1. The starting-price odds for the Frankie accumulator were 25,095-1. But backing a jockey through the card – that's a mug's bet. No person who sees himself as a serious – or even a moderately intelligent – gambler would touch it. Especially when the horse in the last race is a no-hoper. So this was a day for the mug punter: the day when the sheer fools who love the taste of a small bet took a prolonged and terrible revenge on the bookmakers. Some of the bookies had to go out of business. It is estimated that the industry lost £30 million that day: seldom can so devastating a loss have brought forth so much unbridled joy. Frankie had done it for the mugs: for us.

I met Dettori a few years later. I went to his place in Newmarket. Away from the lights and the action and the crowds, he was in a morose mood. It was instantly clear that this was a man with a dark side, with a difficult nature. He tells in his autobiography that after the afternoon of Frankie's Magnificent Seven – for so it was always called – he celebrated by having a row with his wife.

Dettori opened the door to me, with such a scowl on his face that I didn't recognise him. I almost asked him if Mr Dettori was in; I was a beat late in realising that I was already speaking to him. Strangely, I liked this sombre, re-flective, slightly bitter mood. He talked about his disastrous ride on Swain, when, reaching for his whip with too much enthusiasm, he compromised the chances of the brilliant and deeply game horse at the Breeders Cup Classic in the United States. He summed the occasion up rather neatly, I thought: "Everybody fucks up. But me, I fuck up in the biggest fuckin' race in the 'ole fuckin' world." I was deeply intrigued by this second Frankie, adding layers of complexity to the happy-go-lucky cartoon Italian – like Captain Bertorelli in *'Allo 'Allo* – that he showed to the public.

He had a near-death experience in 2000, when the light aircraft he was taking out of Newmarket crashed on take-off, killing the pilot. He was dragged clear from the burning plane by his fellow passenger, the jockey Ray Cochrane, who then went back to try and get the pilot. Dettori had broken an ankle and couldn't move. He subsequently talked about living "life number two".

When he recovered, he went back to racing, and I was there for his return at the Newmarket July course, where he duly won his first race back and gave a press conference. Afterwards, he came up to me to thank me for a piece I had written about him: a courtesy rarely afforded. So yes, a man I like, as well as a heroic deliverer of perfection.

I was in Dublin for the weekend of Frankie's Magnificent Seven, covering the Gaelic football for some reason best known to the sports editor of the time. I remember discussing the day's racing with a taxi-driver. "I knew it was going to be a jockey's day. I just had that feeling. So – I backed Pat Eddery through the card." A snort. "I'll not back that focker again."

36. Pete Sampras

I HAD BEEN WRITING about sport for *The Times* for many years. I was deep into double figures, well into the teens, and the beginning of the third decade was not far off. It's a lot of time to be writing about anything. If you spend a lot of time concentrating a lot of energy on a single subject, the subject changes with the passage of time. You begin to understand it in a different way. You see things you hadn't seen before; you begin to like things that didn't impress you previously; you find heroes where you would once have found people, and dull people at that.

There were times when I found these changing views running in direct opposition to popular taste: I wasn't, after all, writing for people who had spent getting on for 20 years thinking and writing about sport. This can be dangerous for a journalist, whose job is intimately connected to what the readers want to read. But time and again, I found myself swimming against the popular tide when it came to Pete Sampras. Pete Sampras was, in the general view, "boring". I was increasingly inclined to take a hoity-toity line about this: if you find excellence boring then why are you bothering with sport? Why not take on something that's more your size?

But there is something boring about excellence. Excellence tends to lack drama. It lacks teetering, knife-edge excitement. Above all, it lacks uncertainty. When sport is entertaining, it is generally because you don't know what happens next. But when you get a player of Sampras's level of excellence, a great deal of that uncertainty goes. It would be more entertaining to see two mediocrities going at it hammer and tongs than to see Sampras effortlessly blowing the latest hapless opponent away. But I was beginning to find something better than entertainment. I found it in all sports, but most particularly I found it with tennis and with Sampras.

Sampras, people complained, had no character. True, he was not demonstrative. He seldom celebrated the winning of a big point, and seldom looked dismayed when losing one. The air around him remained unpunched. There was one tiny gesture that hinted at the ferocity he unleashed: in his routine before serving, he would brandish his racket, give it an almost imperceptible little shake. Once the ball was in play, there was only one thing he did that had anything flashy about it. It was a shot that gained the nickname the slam-dunk, and it became a signature shot: a leaping smash that hit the ground just the other side of the net and rose with unplayable steepness into the stands. Even that was a functional shot rather than a piece of show-boating. Everything else he played, however brilliant, was stripped down, no-nonsense and strictly for business.

His method was simple: almost grotesquely lacking in elaboration. He served brilliantly, and with great disguise. The serve was reckoned to be his finest shot, but that is wrong. His second serve was his best shot: almost as powerful as his first, and very, very rarely going adrift. It was almost as hard to score points on the second serve as the first. It was the excellence of this second serve that freed him to give everything to his devastating first. And then – if the ball came back – the volley. Once Sampras had taken up his position at the net, he could put away almost any ball that came back. He followed his own serve and he would often come in on his opponent's serve: crowding, brutalising, pulverising. He had fine forehand ground-strokes, so opponents would routinely feed his backhand, often to find Sampras running around the ball to hit a crushing forehand.

Between 1993 and 2000 he lost only one match at Wimbledon. That was in the quarter-finals of the 1996 tournament, when he went out to the eventual and still disbelieving winner, Richard Krajicek. That is to say, he won the title seven times in eight years. My favourite was 1999.

That year was notable for a huge public yearning for the romantic Wimbledon double: Steffi Graf was in the women's final, André Agassi in the men's. They were now an item. Agassi, recovering from the depths of a 141 ranking, was playing the best tennis of his life; he had won the French Open, he was to go on and win the US Open that year; all that and Steffi too. Everyone wanted the tale. *The Times* head of sport, Keith Blackmore, was mad for it, envisaging the most glorious of front-page pictures. He said Sampras was boring. How can you claim to understand sport if you find excellence boring? I asked him, by no means for the first time. (Keith might well have asked me how I could claim to understand journalism when I found a story like the Agassi–Graf Wimbledon weekend unsatisfactory.) Lindsay Davenport spoiled the fun by beating Graf in the women's final, but Agassi was still the popular choice for the men's final the following day. At least he wasn't boring.

Agassi came out and played perhaps the best tennis of his life. He was genuinely brilliant. The only thing that spoiled the day for him was that Sampras went beyond such tawdry stuff as brilliance. Sampras got very close to perfection. He beat Agassi 6-3, 6-4, 7-5. The match was decided in five games in which, if Sampras was not perfect, he was but a fagpaper away. They spanned the first and the second set. From love-40 on his own serve, Sampras reeled them all off: and now, a break up in the second set, he was unstoppable. "I was on fire. It was as well as I can play, quite simply," Sampras said afterwards.

Agassi said: "He hasn't played great all year, then he comes here and wins Wimbledon."

That was Sampras's 12th grand-slam singles title, which brought him level with Roy Emerson at the top of the all-time list. He beat Emerson's record the following year, when he won Wimbledon again. Then it all started to go wrong. The following year Sampras lost at Wimbledon to a young player called Roger Federer. The year after, 2002, he played George Bastl, a Swiss journeyman ranked 145, in the second round. And Sampras started to lose. He was a man in crisis. At each changeover, he read and reread a letter written to him by his wife Bridget. An alert *Times* photographer, Gill Allen, took an over-the-shoulder shot of the letter, but the decision was made, quite rightly, not to publish it, because it was private correspondence.

Sampras went into the US Open that year in some disarray. And won the damn thing, his 14th grand-slam title. In his euphoria, he gave *The Times* permission to print the picture of the letter. It was written in block capitals, addressed to "MY HUSBAND 7 TIME WIMBLEDON CHAMPI-ON... YOU TRULY ARE THE BEST... YESTERDAY IS BEHIND YOU..." Sampras left his time of weakness behind him to find one last chunk of glory. He never played another match.

He was, then, a man of great emotion after all. It was just that on court, he mostly set emotion aside. He reduced himself to the pure essence of victory. He won that 1999 final against Agassi with a second-serve ace. In the press conference afterwards, someone asked: "What was going through your mind when you were making that second serve?" After a pause, Sampras answered: "There was absolutely nothing going on in my mind at that time."

You can keep your entertainment. You can keep your characters. Give me a hero that brings pure, undiluted excellence. That is the highest thing in sport, and those that bring it are the most impressive people in sport's panheroikon.

37. Mark Todd

WHICH SPORTS STAR WOULD you most like to be? There are many ways of playing this splendid parlour game. The first is to look for the greatest and most glorious experiences available in sport, experiences way beyond your capacity, your nerve, your possibilities: to be a ski-jumper, a pole-vaulter, a gymnast. Another is to look at the performers who seem to have something magical about them, whose abilities seem to contradict the basic laws of physics and biomechanics: David Gower with a cricket bat or George Best with a football. These are all high and distant dreams, and the impossibility of realising them is the very point of dreaming them. But you can instead start with the sport you are most capable of doing, and think of that sport's finest performer: thus the golfer covets the abilities of Tiger Woods, the car enthusiast the skill of Ayrton Senna, the cyclist the acceleration of Chris Hoy. This way of thinking makes the skills of these extreme performers almost accessible. It seems that there is some way in which these truly exceptional people are just like you, only more so.

If we are to play by this rule, then I must have Mark Todd. Riding horses is the only sporting activity in which I have ever been competent. I have competed in dressage, showjumping, cross-country and eventing. And if I wasn't frightfully good, I was at least good enough to do it: and I am good enough to keep and ride horses to this day. Todd was the greatest competitive horseman I have ever seen. Todd was an eventer: and the three-day event is the most searching and beautiful of all sports. He was the ultimate sporting expression of what I aspired to in sport. If I look for a super-me in this collection of heroes, I can find him in Todd.

Todd is a lanky New Zealander with a sleepy manner, an extraordinary and instantaneous ability to click with a horse, and a deeply hidden but quite implacable competitive urge. He is the most successful eventer in history, with two individual Olympic gold medals, three Badmintons, five Burghleys and three world championships.

The beauty of eventing is that it is a test of a relationship. It is a sport based on trust. To build a mutual trust with a horse – a trust tested in the most exacting circumstances the human mind can conceive – is the work of years. The aim of eventing is to create a team of two: a team that crosses the boundary of species. An eventer doesn't get on or off horses like a jockey: he finds horses, makes them, schools them, improves them, knows them. A horse-and-rider team at a top-level event is the work of years. Without trust it is nothing: the horse must trust the rider not to ask him to do something impossible. A horse must believe that if he is asked to take off into what looks like nothing, there will be a safe landing on the far side; the rider must trust the horse to jump, not to falter at the last minute and dump him. The commitment with which you ride at a fence depends on trust: without that trust, the horse will sense your lack of commitment and lose commitment himself.

I have known both experiences, commitment and holding back, known them with immense precision. Every cross-country course is designed to test that trust to the limit. There is a type of fence called the rider-frightener: a simple enough fence that looks like a leap into the abyss. If the rider transmits any apprehension to the horse, the horse will stop dead. Other combinations of fences are designed to test the horse's

236

ability to obey precise instructions under intense pressure. Such an extreme test – the sort of test offered by the immense four-star courses of Badminton and Burghley – will ask questions about every schooling session you and your horse have ever done.

Todd sat on Horton Point for 20 minutes. Then, over the course of the next few days, he rode the horse to victory at Badminton.

Todd is a phenomenon. I once went into the ten-minute box, where the riders wait for this nerve-racing stretch of time before setting off on the cross-country. I found myself right in front of Todd. I wish I could transcribe his half-awake New Zealand drawl with perfect accuracy: "Unh, hah, Sahm'n." I said hi back, wondering how anybody could be so impossibly relaxed before so extreme and so dangerous a test: how anybody in such circumstances could be so hyper-aware as to notice a slightly known intruder, how anyone could have time for a small courtesy at such a moment.

I remember an occasion in the Badminton press tent, where the horsey journos were gathered to do their stuff. As is customary, we tend to pool quotes and information. Alan Smith, then the *Daily Telegraph*'s man, called out: "Toddy says it's a tricky course this year, but he thinks it will flow." This important observation was greeted with a spontaneous shout of laughter. All courses flow for Toddy.

It was 1994. Todd had a damn good horse for Badminton, Just An Ace. Then a pair of sisters, Ros and Lynne Bevan, sought out Todd at Badminton. They all knew each other of old. The sisters shared an excellent, safe'n'solid eventer called Horton Point, never quite top class, a well-loved family pet who had given them all some great times. Over the years, Todd had given them advice when asked for, walked the course with them, generally been a good chap. And then Lynne broke her collar-bone, so they offered the ride to Todd, who said yes, and did his 20 minutes.

Todd rode him for another 40 minutes to warm up for the dressage test, and that went pretty well, putting the two of them up in the reckoning. The problem was that the horse, a chunky old thing, wasn't terribly fast. He had never completed a cross-country course within the optimum time. Todd doubted if he was physically capable of getting round the cross-country course without time penalties. "I popped Horton Point over a couple of fences on the Friday, but I must say I felt a bit nervous setting out on the cross-country course on a horse I'd ridden for less than two hours," Todd wrote in his autobiography, *So Far, So Good*.

He had walked the course with the Bevan sisters, and they had urged him to take all the fast and direct routes. Todd agreed, thinking privately that he would amend the plan if things started to unravel. But they didn't. Once they got moving out onto the course, Todd saw at once that the horse liked to take a lot of time to set himself for a fence, and that was why he always had time penalties. "I had to force myself to make him keep coming and trust that he knew what he was doing." It sounds simple. It isn't. Todd had to manufacture this trust from virtually nothing. It was courage of a very high order: the sort of courage you could only find in a person able to tune in at a very profound level to a completely unfamiliar horse.

An event is decided on the final day by the showjumping

test. Todd and Horton Point were in the lead as the show-jumping phase began. "Just stay relaxed and don't screw up," the sisters said encouragingly. "Our lives depend on this."

By the time they entered the ring, the errors made by the others meant that Todd and Horton Point could have knocked two fences down and still won. They were clear as they approached the last two fences: "I remember thinking, OK, you knock them if you want to." But Todd and Horton Point won like champions.

It really was a kind of miracle, though it takes a horseman to see the entire point of it. Todd had the ability to get on any horse, understand him, and then persuade the horse to cooperate, and to give the very best of himself. I got to know Todd pretty well in a period when I was writing a weekly column about horses for *The Times*, and we talked on a good few occasions. I have watched him school horses over jumps and on the flat, I have watched him around horses, I have been in horsey groups with him when the inevitable topic has been discussed. And here's what I have learned.

Nothing.

Absolutely nothing. I might as well try and pick up a few tips on guitar-playing from Jimi Hendrix, about playing the Goldbergs from Glenn Gould. Partly this is the nature of horsemanship: the good horseman puts in the correction before the error comes. His corrections are subtle, more or less imperceptible, and pre-emptive.

But it is also because talent at this level is not something that instructs and informs. It is simply not imitable. These skills are not, after all, accessible. I know no more about how it feels to be Mark Todd riding around Badminton, than I know how it feels to soar off a ski-jumping hill or to hit my first ball in Test cricket for four. I am a horseman: but that is no help. The talent is too high to learn from, just as it is too rare to envy. Todd and I are both horsemen: I have no more in common with him than a house-painter has with Rembrandt.

David Gower on the balcony after England's victory in the Ashes in 1985.

Ayrton Senna in his car at the qualifying round of the Italian Grand Prix in 1994. He died the next day in an accident during the race.

Dancing Brave ridden by Greville Starkey, his first jockey. The Brave went on to win the *Prix de L'Arc de Triomphe* with the finest turn of foot ever seen on a racecourse.

Ben Johnson is set in his block for the final of the 100m at the Seoul Olympics in 1988.

Quarterback Joe Montana played for the San Francisco 49ers from 1979 to 1992 but his greatest moment came in the closing seconds of the 1989 Super Bowl.

Steffi Graf during her 'pretty' stage.

Pete Sampras: the dark destroyer of the lawns of Wimbledon.

Left: Intelligent, emotional and irrepressible, Eric Cantona was "the great enabler". Manchester United became national champions thanks to him.

Right: Mike Atherton. He was the only man the team could rely on during a dismal period of English cricket.

Above: Frankie Dettori takes a flying leap from Mark of Esteem after victory in the Queen Elizabeth II Stakes, one of the seven races he won that day at Royal Ascot in 1996.

Left: Florence Griffith-Joyner may have had the profile of a steriod user but never failed a drug test. She was famous for her extraordinary outfits and manicured nails.

Fu Mingxia diving at the 1992 Barcelona Olympics. Unlike many others, she eventually managed to do her sport on her own terms and for herself.

Tim Henman and the famous fist. He may not have won a grand-slam title but he showed great courage in the face of frequent failure.

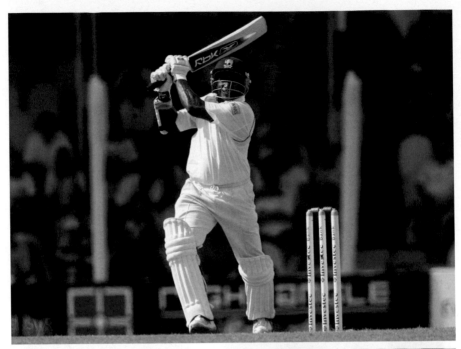

Above: Sanath Jayasuriya led
the maverick Sri Lankan side
to win the 1981 World Cup.

Right: Katarina Witt skated with
certainty, grandeur and majesty. It
won her gold in both the 1984
and 1988 Olympics.

A great sporting moment. Steve Redgrave contemplates the acheivement of his crew in winning the men's coxless four rowing gold medal at the 2000 Sydney Olympics. Redgrave was 38 years old.

Right: Beauty is his weapon of choice. Roger Federer serves against Mark Philippoussis *en route* to winning his first Wimbledon title in 2003.

Left: Andrew "Freddie" Flintoff celebrates taking the wicket of Shane Warne during the fifth Test in 2005.

Jonny Wilkinson kicks the winning goal in the 2003 World Cup final between Australia and England.

Left: Mark Todd wins Badminton on Horton Point, having only ridden the horse for 20 minutes before the event.

Above: David Beckham's is a tale of redemption. He ultimately became a national hero but suffered first as an object of the nation's hate.

Left: Unquestionably a "Great Cricketer", Shane Warne could undermine the confidence of even the best batsmen.

Right: Ellen MacArthur riding the bow of *Kingfisher*, the yacht on which she completed her first solo round the world race.

Usain Bolt boogies to the line in the 2008 Beijing Olympics.

Yelena Isinbayeva shows the power and skill required to execute the perfect L-phase in her record-breaking vault at the 2008 Beijing Olympics.

38. Tim Henman

FAILURE IS AN UNDERRATED heroic trait. Most people just give up. To fail means that you have tried, and that puts you head and shoulders above all those who found giving up the more attractive option. It takes courage to fail. To fail, I mean, while giving everything, while giving your ahhhlll. Anyone can fail while holding a bit back, while refusing to commit the soul and the body to the task in hand. But Tim Henman's commitment was curiously total: so, then, was his failure. He accepted that. Reluctantly, yes, fighting against it every step of the way. But he accepted that the giving of everything was his destiny, and he gave it all without a moment of begrudging. And lost: only to hope again the following year.

Every June brought a rekindling of hope: you know, I really do believe he's going to do it this year. Every July brought ultimate failure: there are a lot of positives I can take from this, I'm still an improving player, I know I'm going to win this tournament one day.

It became an annual ritual. Henman's matches were almost invariably scheduled third-up on Centre Court, the better to catch a big television audience of anxious Brits coming home from work. Every other day, Britain re-entered the long dark teatime of the soul, a phrase I borrowed from Douglas Adams as I continued my annual assignment of covering Wimbledon, my annual assignment of charting the sprouting and blossoming of hope and the tumbling of the fruit in those crucial couple of days before it reached ripeness.

There was, by the end, in some circles, a certain contempt for Henman. This was something I never shared. Henman was seen as a failure because he never won the greatest tournament his sport could offer: we don't regard top foot-ballers as failures because they don't win the World Cup every four years. We salute them for their lesser goals. We never noted Henman's lesser goals, 15 ATP tour titles, his Masters Series win, his fourth place in the world rankings. Henman was also reviled for being "too middle class". For some reason that was seen as acceptable criticism; you don't often find people reviling Wayne Rooney for being "too working class".

Henman was also criticised for being insufficiently passionate. This was a totally astounding view. He was a man seething with passion. It wasn't passion he was short of, it was the ability to express it. Henman is the only player ever to have been disqualified from Wimbledon, and that was for a crime of passion. This was in 1995, when he reacted to his own unforced error by slamming a tennis ball as hard as he could. It struck a ballgirl on the head. He did a public apology and a photo-shoot with the startled girl. It was a bit of a story, it being Wimbledon and all, but back then, Henman was just another losing Brit.

Losing Brits. Losing Brits with wild cards. When *The Times* sends its team to Wimbledon, some unlucky person always gets the job of Plucky Brits Correspondent, with the task of completing a round-up of British first-round losers. Busiest job of them all, we joke every year. Lord, when a British player got into the second week, what a tale that used to be. The idea of a British player actually winning was absurd.

In 1996, Henman beat the number five seed, Yevgeny Kafelnikov, in the first round. There was not an atom of fluke about it. He mixed a spiteful serve with dashing and athletic volleying. He also had the greatest skill in tennis: the ability to surf the emotion of the occasion and to find his best shots for the biggest points of the match. Right from the start, it was clear that Henman could raise his game to astonishing levels: stand toe to toe with the finest in the sport and give them one hell of a game. In the bar afterwards, we all wagged our heads in delight: this guy could really be a top 20 player. You know, I think he has the game to be top ten. He did still better: that's failure? Well, yes it is: but it is also a triumph.

I watched and wrote about Henman for year after year, for Wimbledon after Wimbledon. Another day, another tea-time, another Henman piece. I grew deeply familiar with his mannerisms. The little skip as he walked back down the centre line when particularly pleased with a winning volley. The little fist-pump he did, always below waist level, no doubt because to show more emotion would be vulgar. His base-line prowl, muttering obscenities, in a manner that pained his very proper mother and father when the microphones were turned up.

I knew, with deep intimacy, the rhythm of his matches. He would cruise into a two-set lead, and then take a brief holiday for a couple of games and find himself a break down. Nothing was ever straightforward. There was scarcely a match without its portion of agony.

He reached the Wimbledon semi-finals on four occasions. The first two times he lost to Pete Sampras. The second, in 1999, he took the first set and played the best I ever saw of him. It was a shockingly brilliant display, and I truly felt, for getting on for an hour, that this time, Henman would rise up to another level and take the match and the tournament. But alas, Henman didn't have that raise. The one thing he always lacked on court was authority. He was hopeless at playing the flat-track bully against the lesser players: there were times when higher-ranked players oppressed him purely by means of their position on the dominance hierarchy. But losing to Sampras at Wimbledon was never a disgrace. Sampras had the raises: ultimately, Henman did not.

Henman's year was 2001, when he played Goran Ivanisevic in the semis. Ivanisevic was playing on a wild card, and found his eccentric best in that tournament. All the same, this was Henman's opportunity: the chance to strike in between the eras of Sampras and Roger Federer: the chance to make his mark between god and god. Alas, he was unable to do so. Their semi-final was beset by rain delays, and lasted over three days. Ivanisevic, notoriously nervy, coped better than Henman, and went on to win the tournament, beating Pat Rafter in the final, as Henman himself might well have done. Perhaps should have done.

This strange pattern of annual hope and annual dis-appointment eventually caused some people to resent Henman, but it was hardly his fault that we had hoped for too much from him. He gave all he had. After each annual fail-ure, he would come back to try again, without any reduction in commitment, and once again weave a spell of anguish over the nation.

Henman doesn't make it to this panheroikon in spite of his failure. He makes it because of his failure. Yeats wrote a poem entitled "To a friend whose work has come to nothing". This friend, Yeats said, was "bred to a harder thing than triumph". The poem concludes:

> Be secret and exult,
> Because of all things known
> That is the most difficult.

39. Sanath Jayasuriya

A PLACE THAT YOU visit and love can become part of you: a new homeland for your soul. The great things you find on your travels inspire powerful feelings for the country you found them in. Naturally, that can be expressed in sport: a new loyalty, a new patriotism, one without guilt or need for apology. Thus I find myself cheering for Paraguay and for Zambia at football, and especially, for Sri Lanka at cricket. A fine athlete from a beloved place can easily take on a heroic aspect.

I went to Sri Lanka in 1981, the year that Sri Lanka became a Test match nation. It was also the year that Ian Botham won the Ashes: I had an awful lot of conversations about the greatness of cricket and of cricketers and the daunting prospect faced by Sri Lanka as they prepared to step in against the big players.

It was a glorious trip. I was there for a couple of months. I came back with a deep love of the place, with the effects of a damascene experience that altered my life for ever – namely, with a reawakening to the wild world and its creatures, with a raft of rather hefty stories that I subsequently sold, with new friends, especially Nalin Wijesekera, a maverick journo and professional black sheep of his family, and with a wife. Life was radically changed, all for the better and all with the help of Sri Lanka.

I travelled everywhere on that island. I even went to the supposed no-go areas in the far north, to Jaffna, where the Tamil Tigers hid away, and where the great library had recently been torched by rioting policemen. A civil war is the most painful war of all, and as always, no one barring a few well-armed lunatics wanted its continuation. I stayed among people weary of strife, at a time when the strife had hardly begun. I felt deep empathy with a place and a people that had so many fine and enviable things, and so much unenviable trouble. I went everywhere and met nothing but kindness and welcome and humour and wildlife and beauty and long conversations about cricket.

So naturally, as Sri Lanka started to play cricket in the big league, I shouted my best for them. I hated the way England were so begrudging, occasionally offering them a single Test match, as if Sri Lanka were scarcely worth bothering with: tossing them the occasional crumb, not because they wanted to but because they couldn't get out of it. I thought that one day, Sri Lanka might have something to surprise England with, and perhaps sooner than England realised.

Because I loved the maverick streak in Sri Lanka. I found it, obviously, with Nalin, witty, cynical, adroit and a lover of political mischief-making. He maintained a huge stable of clients, magazines that operated across Asia and the world, and which paid in delicious dollars. I fixed him up as Sri Lanka correspondent for *Asian Building and Construction* – hard to believe, perhaps, but I was the magazine's Hong Kong correspondent at the time – though my personal favourite among his clients was an international seafood magazine. It took rare genius to find that one. Nalin was an Asian gonzo journalist who had never read Hunter S. Thomson. He and his wife Indrani put me up, and my future wife Cindy as well, for days at a time, every time we lurched back into Colombo and prepared for another wild trip to another part of the island.

That maverick streak was part of Sri Lanka's approach to

cricket. It was visible in the independent-minded and frequently argumentative cricketers, who seemed to have no appropriate notion of the need for humility in the face of the older cricket nations. And so we got to the World Cup of 1996, which was to be held in Pakistan, India and Sri Lanka. Australia, a nation that feels that the best way to deal with terrorism is to give in to it, decided not to play their group matches in Sri Lanka in case they got blown up by the Tamil Tigers: the West Indies cravenly followed suit. The Tigers plumed themselves mightily on this donated triumph; there was no trouble in Sri Lanka during the World Cup.

Sri Lanka were underdogs in every possible way. The chance of winning glory by staging matches on home soil had been taken away from them. The chances of a small island making a serious impact on a global competition were rated at something pretty close to zero. The tournament began. Its format was 50-over matches, with fielding restrictions in place for the first 15 overs. Sri Lanka began by scoring 90 runs in the first 15 overs against Zimbabwe.

Back then, that was ridiculous, absurd, impossible. The conventional wisdom was that you batted the opening overs cautiously, kept wickets in hand and were therefore in a position to launch a finely judged acceleration towards the end. Sri Lanka began flat out. But, well – that was only Zimbabwe, wasn't it? Freak result.

The second match was against India. The big boys from the billion-peopled democracy across the water. The real cricketers, World Cup-winning cricketers. Sri Lanka scored 117 in their first 15 overs – 42 in the first three – stats that made the cricket world blink. Sanath Jayasuriya, attacking from the first ball, scored 79 from 76 balls. Jayasuriya was cricket's first pinch-hitter; the name, borrowed from baseball, and inaccurately at that, was subsequently used in one-day cricket to mean an opening batsman with permission to attack. Single-handedly, Jayasuriya changed the competition, and while doing so, changed cricket. He slapped the ball over the infield, taking the aerial route again and again in defiance of popular wisdom. His speciality was a swatted six over cover point: audacious in conception and execution. The combination of fielding restrictions and the flat wickets of the subcontinent made such an approach logical: but it required immense daring. You could so easily look a fool: not just Jayasuriya but the entire country – a country that was struggling to earn respect both as a proper cricketing nation and as a grown-up political one.

But the Sri Lankans dared. They hammered another 123 off the first 15 overs against Kenya, with Jayasuriya making 44, and that got them to the quarter-finals against England.

There was no doubt where my allegiance lay. I felt that England, mean-spirited and conservative, would get their come-uppance: and that they would deserve it. Sri Lanka were my boys: Sri Lanka was my place. Call this phenomenon allopatriotism: loyalty to a country not your own.

Jayasuriya did us proud. England was and is a nation of pawky and often fearful cricketers, a nation that tends to wake up to new trends – especially if they are in cricket – some time after the rest of the world. And they were overwhelmed. England found themselves in the position of the master of aerodynamics who proved conclusively that a bumble-bee can't fly, while the Sri Lankans spread their wings and buzzed off. England made 235 in their 50 overs, with Mike Atherton making 22. Sri Lanka were more than halfway there in the 13th over, when Jayasuriya was out after scoring 82 in 44 balls. Such hitting was unknown in serious cricket. Sri Lanka knocked the rest off with more than nine overs to spare. It was a rout.

Sri Lanka then beat India in Calcutta in the semi-finals. The Sri Lankans lost their first three batsmen, Jayasuriya included, in jig-time, but still put up a decent total. Jayasuriya took three wickets as India collapsed in reply, setting off a riot in the disappointed crowd. That left the final. Sri Lanka's opponents were Australia. Australia has got through to the knock-out rounds despite boycotting their Sri Lanka obligations, because the competition was ill-conceived and bloated, being set up to maximise revenue rather than sporting excellence. Australia set a decent total of 241, and Sri Lanka chased it. Jayasuriya was out early again, but Sri Lanka made it for the loss of just three wickets. Sri Lanka, gloriously and almost absurdly, were world champions.

It wasn't all good. Jayasuriya's fireworks changed the way cricket has been played ever since. One-day cricket, and subsequently Twenty-20 cricket, became slanted in favour of batsmen. Big hitting on flat wickets is now the standard fare. The balance between bat and ball has changed drastically, and the game has become somewhat one-dimensional and acquired a rather tedious showbiz glamour. These days, televised cricket, especially on the subcontinent, is all sixes and adverts.

But never mind that now. Jayasuriya dared to try something new. Jayasuriya dared to fail, Jayasuriya dared to look the most titanic fool in cricket, and his nation dared to look like a bunch of naïve idiots. They stuck to their maverick tradition: for it is only by means of such things that a small nation can make its mark in a big world. The tradition continues, and in cricket, it has brought Muttiah Muralitharan. Muralitharan is a Tamil, a member of the island's minority race; he is also a national hero. His innovative bowling allowed him to become the highest wicket-taker in Test history. His bowling is legal and utterly vindicated, despite continuing grousing and begrudging, mostly from Australia. The mavericks continue to emerge, with the round-arm expresses of Lasith Malinga and the finger-flicking spin of Gehan Mendis. Jayasuriya remains a hero of one of my Other Countries, the man who, by daring to be a fool, not only won but changed everything.

40. Katarina Witt

THIS WAY, LOVE! Look this way! Give us a smile, love! Closer, closer! Laughin' eyes, love! 'Scuse me, love, do you mind taking your top off?

The figure on the ice ceased for a moment to glide. With eyes not laughing, she said: "I am an athlete. I am taking part in a sport. I wear sports clothes."

Thus Katarina Witt silenced a scrum of photographers at Queens ice rink in London: a trim figure in black leggings and a neat little hooded top that she wouldn't remove. She didn't need to remove clothes to take the eye. The skates she wore burned on the ice, her own person beggared all description, age would not wither her, nor custom stale her infinite variety; other women cloy the appetites they feed, but she made hungry where most she satisfied.

Oh yes, she was lovely all right. It would be impossible – not to say dishonest – to write about Witt without mentioning her beauty, for it was not incidental to her achievement. But it is equally false to write only of her physical appearance. She was a performer who was able to go far deeper than laughin' eyes and a hint of cleavage.

I have given myself a hard job here. I must try and skate between Scylla and Charybdis: between the right-on I'm-no-sexist truth and my unavoidable awareness of the phwoar-what-a-scorcher reality. To make a hero of a woman who exploited her bravura sexuality without compunction must also raise certain questions: let us try and address them without prejudice.

I remember, years ago, talking to a brilliant up-and-coming skater, American by birth, Chinese by race. Her career was later ruined, alas, by injury. And she said: "I don't want people to say she's going to win, she's got a triple this, she's got a triple that. I want people to see me just skate past and say: wow, there goes a champion." What this girl dreamed of, Witt achieved.

Witt was born in East Germany. She skated at her kindergarten, she competed at seven and, showing alarming promise, was taken to Karl-Marx Stadt – now back as Chemnitz again – to be trained. She was taken into the maw of the East German sporting machine, and being gifted with rare talent and still rarer competitive toughness, she thrived in this unforgiving atmosphere. She went on to win gold medals at the Winter Olympic Games in 1984 in Sarajevo and in 1988 in Calgary. She won the world championship four times.

Her greatest performance was probably the one in the long programme in Calgary. The Americans were mad to beat her, and believed they had the answer in Debi Thomas. Thomas was tall for a figure skater, black, very athletic, a competitor from the kick-ass silver-medal-goes-to-the-first-loser school of American sport. She went out there to win, and if winning took artistry, then she was even willing to try a bit of that. She went out to nail those jumps and please that crowd. Witt had a different approach. All the same, it was Thomas who was leading the field after the short programme at the Calgary Games. It was hers to lose.

Their rivalry was called the Battle of the Carmens, since both chose to skate to music from the same opera. This was not the most amazing coincidence of all time: Bizet is the default choice of music in skating and gymnastics, in the hope that some really rousing music will elevate second-raters into medal contenders. Thomas said that the difference between the two Carmens was that "her Carmen dies. Mine doesn't". That's not how it worked out.

Here we have to take a pause to remember how figure skating works. Competitors must not only skate beautifully and stylishly and "artistically", they must also perform a series of extremely difficult manoeuvres, manoeuvres which no skater can bring off one hundred times in one hundred attempts. Figure skating is about getting it right on the big occasions: about landing those triple jumps, not in the practice session and during training, but at the final of the Olympic Games. Witt said it was a sport. She was right.

Thomas went out onto the ice after exchanging stinging palm-slaps with her coach, and then choked comprehensively. She missed three of the five triples she had planned in her routine. Her Carmen died.

Witt's performance was not flawless: she missed one of her five triples. But she did more than land a few jumps. She skated with complete certainty, with grandeur, with majesty. She skated as if no one else had a right to be on the ice. She skated as if no one else was competing. She skated with conviction, bringing powerful emotions into the performance. One of the reasons she was able to do this was that her balance was so extraordinarily good. As a result she could use her arms balletically, rather than as mere balancing poles. All skaters must fight against the stiffness of the arms that the need for balance on a precarious surface often brings: Witt danced, and danced as if all the tragedies of the world were upon her. She skated as if she had to express the ultimate concept of womanhood to the world.

If Ian Botham's feats in the Ashes of 1981 were a triumph

of machismo, Witt's victory in Calgary was a triumph of feminisma. If Botham's deeds set him on the top of the male dominance hierarchy, then Witt's performance put her at the top of the female equivalent in her own sporting world. She skated past: she was, quite clearly, the champion.

As a point of information, I should say here that Witt didn't actually win the long programme: that went to Elizabeth Manley of Canada. But Witt had done enough for the gold medal.

After that, she turned professional, a remarkable achievement of persuasion in those days before the Berlin Wall fell. She skated with Brian Boitano in the States and scored a great success. It was then that the Olympic rules were changed, and professionals were no longer barred from Olympic competition. Witt came back for the Winter Olympic Games of Lillehammer in 1994; so, incidentally, did Torvill and Dean. Witt no longer had the jump, alas. The technical tricks had gone. She skated a bravura "Robin Hood" short programme, and then, quite beautifully, to "Where Have All the Flowers Gone". But without the big jumps, she finished seventh. This is, after all, a sport.

Witt, of course, had it both ways, playing the sporting card when convenient, and using her beauty quite shamelessly when it was useful. She did, after all, pose for *Playboy*. In press conferences, she would respond to a question by looking the questioner in the eye and smiling, a smile that turned her eyes into half-moons. Laughin' eyes, love. I know, I tried it. It was rather like swallowing a large Jack Daniels all in one go, ice cubes and all.

But that isn't why she was great, and that isn't why she

makes it into this panheroikon. She is here because she was able to take a great occasion and make it her own: with beauty, art, ferocious competitiveness, finely trained athleticism, grace, elegance, sexuality and an overwhelming desire to be first. It is – did I mention this? – a sport.

2000s

41. Steve Redgrave

IF EXCELLENCE CAN BE considered boring by observers, what about the participants? How do they view the level of work that sustained excellence requires: day after day, a life dedicated to a single thing, a thing to which all other things are second best? Rowing is notoriously demanding on both the body and the mind. It requires long, hard work in the early morning on a river; demanding enough in summer, this is toughness itself in the winter. All oarsmen, at least those who train in Britain, tell tales of the water freezing on their clothes. And then there is the endless land work in the gym, the weights, the ergonometer. Beyond that, there is simply everything else in life: the fact that every waking and every sleeping minute of every day has some kind of relevance – is ultimately dedicated – to the task of winning. For an Olympic rower, that means the task of winning once in four years. Oh, there are staging posts on the way, world championships and so forth, but they are as nothing compared to the Olympic Games. You must sustain an intolerably high level of performance and reach a peak every time the year is divisible by four. Steve Redgrave did that for 20 years, and in the process he won five gold medals at five successive Olympic Games.

In *Casanova's Chinese Restaurant*, the fifth book of Anthony Powell's *A Dance to the Music of Time*, a louche gathering of bohos are discussing Casanova in the eponymous Chinese restaurant. 'Think of having to listen to his interminable tales about girls. I could never get through Casanova's *Memoirs*. Why should he be considered a great man just because he had a lot of women? Most men would have ended by being bored to death.'

'That is why he was a great man. It wasn't the number of women he had, it was the fact that he didn't get bored.'"

It wasn't – or it wasn't just – the number of gold medals that Redgrave won. It was also the fact that he didn't get bored. The point about Redgrave was that he was never sated. He distilled the entire range and meaning of sport into to a hunger for victory, and with it, an addiction to the process of getting there.

A member of the Cambridge crew of the Boat Race of 2010 said: "Rowing is meant to be boring. I read that Baron de Coubertin [the founder of the modern Olympic Games] thought that rowing was the perfect sport for his new Olympics because it was so bad for spectators. It was worth doing simply for sport's sake, not because anyone might want to watch it."

Entertainment is a mere bonus in sport. Sport is not supposed to create entertainers; it is supposed to create heroes. If you want entertainment, look to reality TV and soap operas. Any footballer, any cricketer, any professional athlete of any kind who declares "I see myself as an entertainer" should be sacked on the spot. Similarly, anyone who says that sport is "part of the entertainment business" should be barred from any involvement in sport for the rest of his life, including spectating.

Sport is much better than entertainment. And in those five, perhaps rather dull expeditions along 2,000 metres of open water – and a rowing lake is usually a hugely dull piece of landscape – put together over 20 years of extortionately demanding and often excruciatingly tedious preparation, Redgrave's quintuple victory is one of the most remarkable achievements in the history of sport.

He won as a member of the coxed four at the Olympic Games of 1984 in Los Angeles. In Seoul, he won the coxless pair with Andy Holmes. The two subsequently got divorced, and there was an arranged marriage with a hulking, grinning Old Etonian named Matthew Pinsent. Redgrave is fiercely dyslexic and gained a single O level – woodwork – after his time at a comprehensive school. Redgrave was all blazing intensity: Pinsent was full of smirking little quips. Obviously they got on. Redgrave learned how to lighten up when it was necessary: Pinsent found an answering intensity.

They won the pairs in 1992 in Barcelona and then again in Atlanta in 1996. It was after this race that Redgrave famously said, as the boat glided to the dock after the gold medal row: "Anyone who sees me in a boat again has my permission to shoot me."

But of course, as soon as he stopped, he missed it. Perhaps he missed the training, the routine of pain, the security of what he knew. Perhaps he missed the hunger. Perhaps he felt that doing something remarkable was not enough, when he might be able to do something unique. So back he went into training, this time in a four, with Pinsent at stroke. He contracted diabetes: learned how to deal with it. Over the years, Redgrave crews acquired an aura, a mystique: they were never beaten. But then Redgrave's four suffered a devastating defeat in a World Cup regatta at Lucerne, a few weeks before the Olympic Games. The mystique had gone. Surely, one more victory, with Redgrave now 38, was too much to ask?

I was there at the lake, there when the Italian crew flashed passed them in the last few strokes and I groaned in despair even while wondering what the hell I was to write – and why the hell were those people cheering and waving the Union flag? It was then I realised that the angle had deceived me: Redgrave and his boys had hung on. They won by 0.7 seconds, completing one of the most remarkable sporting journeys.

He did retire after that one.

Redgrave is always referred to as an "Olympian". This word is used far more sparingly of other great performers at the Olympic Games. Perhaps this is because there is something mountainous about Redgrave: in his size, in his unyielding nature. Perhaps it's also because he is so obviously a mythological character: taking part in a stripped-to-the-bone narrative, from which only his uncompromising view of the world is made clear. All the heroes in this book have different aspects of the heroic about them: Redgrave represents the principle itself, with nothing added. Redgrave saw his goal and moved towards it, stepping neither to left nor to right, looking at nothing on either side, however beguiling. Nothing that was not victory was tempting, or even interesting. Redgrave represents the notion of victory in its most basic form: the pure, hard, brutal essence of seeking to be the best, and being prepared to destroy the hopes and dreams of anyone who dares to stand in the way.

42. Roger Federer

DURING WIMBLEDON 2003, a number of eminent people in tennis got together to sort the sport out: ex-players, ex-champions, the great and the good of the game. They were concerned that tennis was losing its magic, its beauty, its subtlety. The problem, as they saw it, was technology: modern rackets were lighter, more resilient and equipped with enormous sweet spots, so that the game required less skill. The game, these people felt, was being taken away from ball-players and handed to strength-and-endurance athletes, grunting artisans who pummelled the ball from the baseline, drilling ball after ball deep and flat, able to run for ever. The rackets, forgiving of minor errors, were creating a new generation of pseudo-players: people who couldn't hope to live with the great names of the past, if they played on a level playing field with antiquated technology. Artistry, they declared, was dying on its feet.

Never can a campaign have fallen so flat so fast. Because Wimbledon 2003 was the tournament at which Roger Federer made his mark. It was clear right from the start that he was likely to be one of the greatest champions of all time: perhaps the greatest of them all.

I was there, covering that tournament, but I didn't get the chance to write about him till his semi-final against Andy Roddick, whom Federer dispatched in straight sets. "Federer yesterday abandoned his conventional racket and replaced it with one he bought at Ollivander's in Diagon Alley," I wrote breezily. "Federer bought his racket where Harry Potter bought his wand." Federer just said: "I really do feel quite good about myself."

It was the beginning. "Federer left the court with his racket

trailing sparks of purple and green, inadvertently transfigur-
ing a ballboy into a toad," I continued, in love with the com-
parison. Federer beat Mark Philippoussis in the final with another detonation of pure brilliance. He wasn't as consistent,
but he played the games at the end of the first set and the
beginning of the second in a trance of complete perfection,
and that is usually enough to win. It certainly was that day.

I was there when the Federer narrative began, and I have
been with it most of the way. I have marvelled at his artistry,
and have explained many times that art is simply his method:
his goal is not beauty but victory. Beauty just happens to be
his weapon of choice.

And yet, as I look here at the heroic aspect of Roger Federer, I can't deny that the desire to create beauty is part of his
nature. Not, I think, at the cost of victory: but the way he
exults in pure shot-making is a fine thing to see, one that
reaches his audiences on a profound level. There is that smug
little smirk that he wears when walking back to the baseline
after a particularly well-struck shot: a little moment of self-
satisfaction that always reminds me of my mother after she
had let forth one of her more devastating verbal squibs.

Federer has always revelled in being different from the
other players. But his talent is so high, he has no need to play
the misunderstood artist, the player who would rather go the
pretty way and lose than win ugly, the player who chooses
to lose because he has higher principles than mere winners.
No: Federer uses the beauty of his shot-making like a club
and belabours his opponents into submission. He exploits his
on-court serenity the same way: let the other person huff and
grunt and sweat; Federer cruises about with a faint smile and

lets his opponent destroy himself. More than any one else I have ever seen in any of the oppositional sports, Federer makes his opponent look as if he were voluntarily submitting to Federer's will. With Federer, as with George Best and David Gower, we find a real completeness to the illusion of complicity.

Being number one has always been a crucial aspect of Federer's talent. There were normal players, and then there was Federer. He held the number one position for 237 weeks at a stretch; no one had done that, or got close. In one period between the summer of 2005 and the autumn of 2007, he took part in ten grand-slam tournaments and won eight of them, losing in Paris to Rafael Nadal in the final on both of the other occasions. He then suffered a bout of glandular fever. That pernicious virus reduced him just a little. Nadal maintained a winning record over him, always beating him on clay, and eventually beating him at Wimbledon in 2009. Every time a case is made for Federer as the greatest ever performer in his sport, room must be made for Nadal, who alone of the tennis players has no fear of Federer.

Federer has taken the ball skills of tennis to a level never seen before. He has used the new technology to design, create and execute a thrilling new range of possibilities. He has half a dozen choices of shots for every ball, because of his unique mixture of eye, hand-skill and imagination. The gorgeous forehand is perhaps the best shot ever seen in any ball game, up there with the Denis Compton cover-drive or the David Gower flick-pull. He has a range of spins and flicks you'd have thought impossible to inculcate with an instrument as unwieldy and downright unsuitable as a tennis racket. Time and again you find yourself watching Federer and bursting into laughter: surely no one should be able to play that shot. Federer's imaginative range confounds everybody, not just those actually playing.

Federer's skills have something anachronistic about them: harking back to a time when players were less fit and less strong. Finesse was easier, because opponents were less mobile. And there is something anachronistic in Federer himself: his gifts are so extravagant and so extraordinary that it is easy to view him with the eyes of a child, as a naïve sports fan who likes to see all great performers in sport as gods. Sport's conventional use of the word hero, in short.

But Federer has shown us his vulnerabilities: his series of defeats to Nadal, his woeful fit of tears after he had lost to Nadal in the final of the Australian Open in 2009, his sometimes too-great air of self-satisfaction, his smug self-portrayal in advertisements, his loss of form – only comparative, it must be said – after his bout with the virus.

All the same, it is harder to see Federer's imperfections than those of most sporting heroes viewed in maturity: perhaps one should make an effort to do so, if only for the sake of one's self-respect. But Federer's brilliance has been so rich and so profound a delight that it is very tempting not to bother: to view this incomparably gifted athlete and wilfully abandon all the critical abilities one has learned over the years. To allow Federer to make us feel young again: naïve, gushing, absurd, humble. It does one good to admire a great man without bothering too much about his self-evident faults and his failings. It is important to feel humble every now and then; important, too, to feel young, or at least, to become reacquainted with our younger selves. Perhaps that is one of the reasons why we need heroes: not just to emulate, but to keep us in our place, to stop us from getting above ourselves.

Federer has outstripped Pete Sampras and therefore everybody else in terms of grand-slam tournaments won, which is the only way to measure success in tennis. But even if someone were to come along and beat his record in terms of numbers, it is unlikely that they would do so by means of such beauty and artistry, such style. Federer really is the greatest of all time. It is not necessary to worship him as a god: but a certain amount of deference is – well, therapeutic.

43. Jonny Wilkinson

THERE WAS ALWAYS A strange quality of innocence about Jonny Wilkinson. He was one of those very rare people who, on believing something, believed in it without compromise. Had he got religion, he'd never have been just a good, solid church-going Christian. He really would have given away all his earthly goods, he really would have given himself up to prayer and good works. Like Ayrton Senna, he'd have been a saint, though a very different kind. Wilkinson lacks the narcissism and the introspection of Senna: a stage-stealing martyrdom would not have been for him. He never sought glory for himself, because he believed too profoundly in the notion of sinking self into a common cause. So sink self he did. All of it.

This total, unblinking, ungrudging commitment made Wilkinson a potentially dangerous man. But he took the course of sport, and it led to the strange glory of an ephemeral victory and a long-term place in the nation's panheroikon.

Wilkinson's notion of life is unyielding. If, for example, you are pretty good at something, then with work, you can probably become very good. But that wasn't enough for Wilkinson. He reckoned that if you could go from very good to very good indeed, and that all it would take would be unending hours of work and a life in which work still count-ed for everything, and in which everything else counted for nothing, then that was what you'd do. Wouldn't everybody?

Well, no, they wouldn't and they don't, but no matter. Wilkinson worked tirelessly at his game, at his strength, at his fitness, at his kicking. He became the England fly-half, the one position on the rugby field that can showcase a star. But Wilkinson had no interest whatsoever in standing out from the rest. He'd seek to do exceptional things because it benefited the team, but to be singled out for praise caused him acute embarrassment. As if people might think that this was why he did it. He did it for the team, for the boys, for the cause. He was no better than the pushers and the shovers and the sprinters and the dodgers. And so when he played, first and foremost he tackled. Small for a rugby player, and though beautifully built, no human battering ram, he could nonetheless tackle like a rat-trap. Didn't mean to hurt anybody, but well, he had to do it for the team. You don't often find the best fly-halves at the bottom of a ruck for half a match, but that was part of Wilkinson's stock-in-trade.

He mastered rugby's eccentric closed skill of goal-kicking: no one to interfere, to help or to hinder: just you and a target. Wilkinson built up an idiosyncratic method, which – quite inadvertently – became an iconic, signature pose: hands clasped before him, head cocked, eyeing the target, universe reduced to a wooden aitch and the sweet spot on a ball. He was remorseless, relentless, merciless. He kicked everything. It got to the point when the opposition didn't dare concede a penalty in their own half, because Wilkinson would invariably kick the three points. That inhibition gave England the space and time they needed to take opponents apart.

And that's what England did, in a brief and glorious period when England dominated world rugby. The team was exceptional in many areas: but it was Wilkinson's kicking, in the inevitable and regular ticking of the scoreboard, that underpinned everything England did. In 2002, they won three autumn internationals against the three southern-hemisphere giants; they were trailing 19-31 to Australia but Wilkinson scored all the points that took England to a 32-31 win. In the following winter of 2003, they won the Six Nations. Then, with the World Cup looming, they had the temerity to travel to Australia and New Zealand for warm-up games. Wilkinson scored all the points as England beat New Zealand 15-13 in Wellington, and they then beat Australia 25-14.

Which brought us to the World Cup and Wilkinson's finest hour. In the quarter-finals, Wilkinson scored 23 points as England beat Wales 28-17; in the semis he scored the lot as England beat France 24-17. Which brought England to the final. This match should have been a straightforward England win, but eccentric refereeing consistently penalised England to Australia's great benefit. The score was 17-17 in the final moments of extra time. It was then that England called for a play they termed "zigzag". Matt Dawson, the scrum-half, made a decisive little dart, Martin Johnson, the incomparable captain, ran into contact to get Dawson out of the ruck and in position to make the pass that counted. Dawson then fired the ball to Wilkinson. That moment was what zigzag was all about.

And time stopped. Wilkinson, with a sweet, nonchalant swing of his right boot – he was naturally left footed – made immaculate contact with the sweet spot on the ball, and up it went, end-over-ending into the Australian night, threading through the giant aitch as if drawn by a mighty force. England had won the World Cup. Jonny had won the World Cup.

It was shortly after this that Wilkinson turned into sport's Job. Sport, having given him so much, decided to take it all back. One injury followed another. Two weeks after the World Cup final, he had a broken shoulder. He had a haematoma on his arm. He tore a medial knee ligament. He then tore it again. He had appendicitis. He then tore a knee ligament, something of a running theme. He also suffered a lacerated kidney. One after another, the misfortunes fell: and Wilkinson was back in rehab again, working, working, never for an instant doubting that he would be back to full health and that it was all worth it.

He became Rehab Man: the only man in England who believed he would play again. No setback seemed to sicken him. Every bit of bad luck made him hungrier for his return. And it was this, as much as his feat in winning the World Cup, that made him so greatly beloved: a man who, once he has started fighting, simply will not stop – certainly not for a ridiculous reason like the inevitability of defeat. As ever, Wilkinson reduced the world to simplicities: to give less than everything is a betrayal of yourself and of everybody else as well. To give less than everything is a form of life-denial. Unthinkable.

And eventually Wilkinson did come back. He played in the World Cup of 2007, though he didn't make the first two matches. He got injured again. But he came back, scoring all the points as England, shockingly, beat Australia 12-10 in the quarter-finals. He then hit a last-minute drop-goal to beat France in the semis. And though England lost the final to South Africa, Wilkinson is the leading point scorer of World Cup history with 241.

Wilkinson inspires a little pity along with the admiration: a feeling that by seeing life in such simple, such downright terms he is missing many of its nuances and subtle joys. But Wilkinson doesn't do nuances. Wilkinson simply gives everything. There is something deeply disturbing about this simplicity: and deeply impressive, too. The giving of everything is something that only exceptional people do. Wilkinson was not just a giver of himself: he was a spendthrift of himself. He became that impossible thing: a superstar without an ego: a hero to whom the concept of being a hero means nothing.

44. Andrew Flintoff

THE HEROIC STATUS OF Andrew Flintoff must, like Tim Henman's, be set in the context of failure. We must consider Flintoff's own failure, both before and after 2005; we must also consider the failure of England cricketers over a period of 18 years. England beat Australia in the Ashes series of 1987. Since then, Australia had won every time. They did so again and again; they did so by massive margins; they did so with relish; they did so with contempt. It was cricket to hide from: cricket to stare at in hideous fascination; cricket to forget: cricket that could never be forgotten.

I was prepared to cheer for Sri Lanka against England, but I was never going to cheer for Australia. There are limits. The pain of all but 20 years of humiliating defeats to Australia cut very deep. The idea of England actually winning an Ashes series was an impossible dream, like believing that the stars are God's daisy chain and that every time a fairy blows its wee nose a baby is born.

The luxuriant fantasy of an Ashes win was intermittently fuelled by promising young players, players who never quite delivered on their promise. Flintoff was one such – yet another New Botham: an all-rounder who, according to the traditional model of the New Botham, never quite bowled or batted well enough.

But England began to improve. Improvement came about because of a potent combination: Duncan Fletcher, the head coach, a planner of great thoroughness and foresight; Nasser Hussain, a captain fearsome in his ambitions for English cricket, who was succeeded at precisely the right time by the less temperamental Michael Vaughan; and the beginning of the system of central contracts, which gave the England coach control of his own players. England began to play like a serious side again: at least, they did when they weren't playing Australia. Year after year, Australia proved that they were as strong a team as has ever played the game; match after match they lined up with some of the finest cricketers of history.

Flintoff was a hugely talented player, so much so that for years, he was able to get by on talent alone. He was soft with himself when it came to training, easy on himself when it came to ambition, a man prepared to do what he thought was his best: secretly preferring to take the easier path. Then came a terrifying meeting with his advisers, one in which he was treated with scathing contempt for what he had achieved, when balanced against his abilities. Flintoff changed his attitude, started to work, discovered hidden layers of ambition, slowly began to believe that he was better than talented. Then came the Ashes series of 2005. And total let-down.

The first Test of the series at Lord's saw all the optimism turn to dust: same old Poms, giving up when the going got tough. Flintoff scored three runs in the match. England surrendered for 180 on the final day. There had been days of rich promise, but it ended in crashing disappointment. England's cricket followers braced themselves for another summer of misery. Failure: failure in the long history of defeat at Australia's hands, failure in the first Test, failure in Flintoff's performance.

Something happened in the 11 days between the first and the second Test. God knows what. Perhaps it happened in the last minute before the match began, in the contemptuous way that the Australian captain, Ricky Ponting, won the toss and asked England to bat. Clearly, he expected another same-old-Poms collapse. He fancied he had before him a demoralised team and he was determined to make the advantage tell. But England responded with intemperate fury. Outrageously, they went on the attack from the first ball, and carried on throughout the day, scoring 407 runs. Flintoff made 68 of them. He made another 73 in the second innings, taking part in a decisive last-wicket partnership with Simon Jones. Flintoff hit nine sixes in the match, an Ashes record. It is very rare for an all-rounder to succeed with both disciplines in the same match: Flintoff also took seven wickets. England won on an extraordinary last day.

The rest of the summer went from drama to drama, with Flintoff at the heart of all of them. He turned the fourth Test at Trent Bridge with a century of murderous purpose. It was an effort of will, rather than one of swashbuckling nonchalance: as if Flintoff had taken on a new personality to suit the needs of his team. The summer ended in glory. The unbelievable was manifestly real: the impossible was made actual before us. It all came down to Flintoff: his nature, his decency, his relish for the challenge, his recently found ambition, his belief that he and his team could beat the best. In that series he scored 402 runs and took 24 wickets. He was the difference between defeat and a quite astonishing prize.

As I mentioned earlier in the Bob Beamon chapter, I have argued about Flintoff frequently with Mike Atherton, in his capacity as *The Times'* chief cricket correspondent. Atherton maintains that Flintoff can't be considered a great cricketer, because the stats don't bear it out, because there are too many blips, because there are too many failures, because there is no consistency, because everything about his record is patchy and hints of a person too easily pleased.

I agree with every word of this. I agree with Atherton's assessment of Flintoff, but not with his definition of greatness. Flintoff was genuinely great, the finest cricketer in the world, for six weeks: and that's enough, because in those six weeks, he was able to bring home something that England had been yearning for over the course of 18 years. It was the conquest of failure: England's and his own.

Nothing in Flintoff's subsequent career lived up to those weeks. He captained England in India and came out with a 1-1 draw in the Test series, which was fairly splendid; he was also captain of England when, as holders of the Ashes, they went to Australia in 2006–7. England were destroyed over the course of five Tests in a desperate revisitation of ancient humiliations. Flintoff's career has involved a number of foolish moments, most of them to do with drink, especially the notorious night-time frolic with the pedalo. His Test match career ended when England beat Australia in the series of 2009. For one brief session in that summer, there was music in the air and we had Flintoff Unbound once again as, in a match-winning spell, he took five wickets at Lord's.

He was not as good as Botham, nor would he claim to be. He was not even as good as he might have been. What's more, he was always that little bit sharp on the commercial opportunity, always that little bit too ready to sport the logo or brandish the product. Flintoff is a hero of the later part of my life: a time when you see the faults of others plainly enough, perhaps more plainly than you are capable of perceiving virtues. Flintoff was in many ways an unsatisfactory cricketer. That is entirely beside the point.

The point of Flintoff is 2005. The point is that Flintoff, in those few summer weeks, turned sporting history on its head and forced cricketing tradition to work backwards. It was Australia who were snappish and uncertain and rent by feuds; it was the Australian captain, Ricky Ponting, who was making an ass of himself; it was the Australian batsmen who were oppressed by crash-hot fast bowling; it was the English who seemed to have the luck, the run of the green, the better of the decisions.

It all centred around Flintoff, simultaneously genial and hostile, deeply at ease with himself in the intensity of Ashes conflict. It was Flintoff who dominated the series, Flintoff who reversed the tide, Flintoff who brought about this great healing of harms. For six weeks, Flintoff was genuinely great. For six weeks, he trod the grass of Old England as a hero.

45. Shane Warne

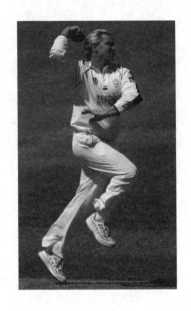

SPORT TENDS TO SUPPORT the Great Man Theory: the notion that history is shaped by a few extraordinary individuals; that the Second World War is all about Churchill and Hitler. We like to look for heroes in real life, that is to say, to turn real life into a narrative that we can easily comprehend. Since every narrative depends on the vividness of its characters, we have a great weakness for peopling real history with semi-imaginary heroes.

Sport creates its own narratives, its own version of reality, and portrays them dramatically, in a kind of exaggerated and fast-forward version of real life. That's why sport is particularly good at bringing us heroes: people who change the outcome of events by an individual assertion of the will. At times, in sport, we seem to see the Great Man Theory played out before us. Sport is, like history, perfectly able to support rival theories: Ed Smith, the former cricketer who played three times for England, discussed this in his excellent book *What Sport Tells Us About Life*, and suggested different and contradictory ways in which the Ashes series of 2005 might have been interpreted by Gibbon, by Carlyle and by a counter-factual historian. But being human, our default option is myth-making, and our natural preference is for Great Men and Great Women. Heroes, in short. In sport, this is almost a legitimate approach, since myth-making is one of the central functions of sport.

Which brings us to Shane Warne, unquestionably a Great Cricketer. I was there to watch him single-handedly, by force of will, take hold of a Test match that was dying on its feet and turn the match, and the entire series that followed, into a rout. It was one of the most devastating things I had ever seen in sport, and certainly the most shattering cricket match I have ever sat through. It took place in Adelaide in 2007.

Warne, the Australian leg-spinner, was a player of brilliance. He had two marvellous complementary talents: he could make the ball spin prodigiously and he could bowl over after spinning over with unyielding accuracy. He was the only practising cricketer to make it to the list of *Wisden's* five cricketers of the 20th century, and that was when he had nearly a complete decade at the top level still to go. He had been bewildering English batsmen for years, starting in 1993 with his first ball in Test cricket in England, a ball that literally turned 90 degrees to beat Mike Gatting. He had all the variations, but more than that, he had a fine understanding and a deep relish of the duel between batsman and bowler. He had the brain to seize on a batsman's weakness and the technique to make the plan work.

He also had a presence, strutting, swaggering, shrewd: a way of somehow implying that he, and he alone, understood cricket and the art of leg spin. He could make batsmen feel inferior to him, even those that did well against him: he could also make umpires feel inferior, less knowledgeable, less capable of judging the flight of a ball than the man doing the bowling, than the man doing the appealing.

But Warne was mostly able to carry all this off with courtesy, with decency, with a righteous delight in the cut and the thrust. Michael Vaughan, England's victorious captain in the Ashes series of 2005, had a glorious tour of Australia in 2002–3 when he scored three centuries. He said: "He was great to face because he gave you respect. If you do well against him, he is not one to give abuse. He will just say 'shot'. And after the game or your innings he will come and say 'well played'."

I met him just once. We shook hands: his hand seems to be all palm, with stubby fingers added as an afterthought. I was conscious of a strange heat, a tingling, as if these were the hands of a healer. He said he had enjoyed something or other I had written: not a courtesy you get every day. I got the feeling that for all his fame, Warne still manages to exist in the real world. But I suspect that he was always confident in giving his courtesies to an opponent, or anyone else for that matter, because, even when bested, he knew without arrogance that he was one of the greatest players that had ever played the game. He was also deeply certain that, even when temporarily beaten, he would win in the end.

That's how it was in 2007. He had taken 34 wickets in the great Flintoff series of 2005, and it is my confident belief that had Warne been captain, Australia would have won a desperately tight series. But he was not captain. There had been too many indiscretions: he served a ban for drugs after using a diuretic; he accepted money from a bookmaker, out of folly and greed rather than corruption; there was a series of sexual scandals. Warne was a loser in 2005, despite being the finest player in a team of Australian greats. This ageing but still brilliant group was still together, more or less, to line up against England in Australia in 2007. More than one had delayed retirement, out of a lust for revenge. It was expected to be a tightly fought series. Australia won the first Test, but England fought back mightily in the second.

On a flat pitch in Adelaide, I watched England compile 551 for 6 declared. Paul Collingwood got a double century; Kevin Pietersen fell for 158 after a spectacular innings, one in which Warne himself was reduced to bowling outside leg-stump, simply bowling where Pietersen couldn't reach it. It was as near as any one has ever seen to Warne running up the white flag. Pietersen said after that he had "mastered" Warne. Australia replied with 513 runs of their own; this really was a horribly easy pitch. On, then, to the final day and a match that was moving sleepily towards a draw.

Warne was the most prominent among those planning to retire from Test cricket at the end of this series. He did not plan to go gently into that good commentary box. And so, by sheer force of will, he created a panic. He induced in England a sudden, dreadful and terminal doubt. It was a landslide started by the first tumbling rock: Warne convinced the umpire, Steve Bucknor, that Andrew Strauss had hit the ball: he had been caught when the ball had, in truth, come directly off the pad. All at once, the England team turned into the cast of *Watership Down*. They went tharn: the term in the book for a rabbit caught in a car's headlights. But it was Warne that dazzled them: Warne's skill, Warne's will. Brett Lee began to find some reverse swing at the other end, but the panic was already there, and it was all Warne's doing. He finished with four wickets. England were all out for 121 because Warne wanted it that way. Australia then knocked off the runs, not without a few alarms, but there was never any doubt. They went on to win the series 5-0: as savage a piece of revenge as it is possible to inflict in the field of sport. Warne's revenge.

It was painful to witness. The following day, I left the tour. Most of my colleagues were bound for Perth and the next Test. I was bound for Sydney and then home, but all passengers were required to join the same snaking queue at the check-in desks at Adelaide Airport. And each time a new shifting of the queue brought me up against yet another cricket writer, I found a person in a state of deep shock. Genuinely traumatised. It was as if we had all witnessed a terrible car accident: the same sense of stunned disbelief. We were all faced with the impossibility of coming to terms with so terrible an event. Sport can do this to people. Warne can do this.

The rivalry between Australia and England is one of the strangest in sport. The Welsh at rugby, and sometimes the Scots at football, will exhibit a genuine hatred for England, matched by an infuriating incomprehension from England. With Argentina and Germany in football, the rivalry with England is fraught, and full of things that do not seem to be forgivable. A history of warfare, just for starters.

But the rivalry between Australia and England is probably even more intense, especially as an Ashes series lasts across days and months. But however deeply the English desire to beat Australia, you don't find English people hating Australians. Nor, very often, save in a few old bigots, do you find Australians hating the English. The time for that is long gone: Australia is a sparkling, independent and successful nation. Most English people who arrive in Australia love the place at once: it has something our own tired nation lacks: a freshness, a sense of being in a country that is still inventing itself, a feeling of infinite possibility. Most Australians love England because England has things Australia lacks: a sense of permanence, of time, of meaning. We are each other's completion, and the relationship, though it is marked out by a great and hugely enjoyable sporting rivalry, has something more akin to love than hate.

As England completed the last rites in the Ashes series of 2005, the Barmy Army, which had been serenading Warne with some unpleasant songs throughout the series, quite literally changed their tune. "Wish you were English – oh yes we wish you were English... wish you were Eng----lish..."

He couldn't have been, of course. Had he been born in England he'd have been somebody else. No person could be more stridently Australian. But his qualities as an opponent made him something more than a figure we must respect. In his fallibilities, his human frailties, his extraordinary talent, his glorious zest for the contest, he was a man who – despite England's deep desire to see him fail – could not be seen as anything other than a hero. His story was, after all, an inextricable part of our story.

46. Fu Mingxia

I WOULD NOT STAND up to defend the grab-'em-young sporting policies of autocratic nations, but the argument against the system is not to be found in the champions it produces. I knew that when I first saw Fu Mingxia: the little waif of Barcelona. She had become world diving champion on the ten-metre board at the age of 12; as a result, the age for elite competition was switched to 14, but not in time to keep Fu out of the Olympic Games of 1992. She was photographed on the high board of the open-air swimming complex on the top of Montjuic: the great cityscape behind her, the confectionery-like spires of the Sagrada Familia unmissable.

She won, and became the perfect image of a great Games. Frail – just five feet tall and seven stone – and with regulation cropped hair, she was, obviously, designed to represent the public face of a great and implacable nation. She played the part, for she knew no other: and yet there was something more. There was a composure, a strength, a sense of an individual will behind that victory. She certainly wasn't going through the routines like one hypnotised. There was something of herself involved. Perhaps there is in all champions.

Fu came from a poor Chinese family, parents a factory worker and an accountant. She went to gymnastics with her older sister, but was diverted into diving: she lacked extreme flexibility, but had grace and courage and agility. One drawback: she couldn't swim. She was to speak later about diving with a rope round her waist, hauled out after every dive. It takes enough courage to dive even if you can swim. She also spoke about her first ascent of the ten-metre board. She was terrified: but it was a rule that no diver should leave the back way. That is to say, by means of the steps. The front exit was the only way down. She jumped.

When she was nine she was taken away from her parents, from her own *sagrada familia*, in a manner unthinkable to us in the West. She trained ten hours a day, seven days a week. This is a system with a high wastage rate, one which treats the losers as expendable. But Fu was not a loser. She had the control, the courage, the desire for success. A diver is required to make each descent as close to the board as possible: Fu regularly brushed the edge of the board with her hair. And her hair was cropped, remember.

Four years after the Barcelona Games, the Olympic Games were in Atlanta and Fu was 17. She had grown two inches and added a couple of stone to her weight: she could now power the springboard. I went to watch her in that event; she had already won the platform diving. Now here's a thing: you can judge diving with your eyes closed. The sport is about control in the air. Control is not complete without a clean vertical entry to the water. As the competition reached its climax, Fu was up there among the leaders. But when it came to the dives that would decide the gold medal, the difference between champion and the rest was made clear. With dive after dive, I could hear the ker-splish and the ker-splash of the crooked entry, the legs making a secondary sound as the diver under or over rotated. Such problems are the direct result of a failure to control the flight. Diving is a very precise business, one that requires an utterly secure nerve. Fu, as champions do, found her best at the point that it really mattered. She hit the water with a single bass thrummmmm.

Diving is a hard discipline. It involves hours of flexibility exercises daily on dry land: those shapes you make in the air must be perfect, in the pike position, face hard against knees. My colleague Craig Lord, trying to humanise this cog in the Chinese sports machine, asked her: "Which exercise do you hate the most?" She gave him a look of contempt: "The only exercise I don't like is one I can't do."

Eyes like two small brown stones.

Magnificent. And so she prevailed on the state to let her retire: the state was changing and the fame of individuals like Fu was one of the reasons it was changing. They couldn't just order her back to work: it wouldn't do. And so Fu went to Qinghua University in Beijing to read economics: "The last thing I wanted to do was dive. I just wanted to be a kid without any pressures." So she was. What's more, for the first time in her life, she could eat what she liked. Inevitably, she got a little stout. Someone asked if she had really been an Olympic champion. I suspect at this question, Fu's eyes changed into two small brown stones.

"It made me realise I loved the sport and could do it on my terms." My terms. The glorious realisation of young people everywhere: self-determination, autonomy. Doubly thrilling in a state that sought control over its citizens, and in particular, over the athletes it chose to represent it. So Fu trained half-days, gave herself weekends off: "Practising for the sake of practice is stupid." Soon, she was good enough to dive for her country again. Good enough to dive at the Olympic Games in Sydney in 2000.

The crop-haired waif was gone. She was a woman all right, with long, streaked hair. She gave interviews without a minder, and no one dared to do anything. She broke curfew — not for crazy drunken exploits, just to point out that she was doing this for herself. I was there in Sydney when she won her fourth gold medal, again on the springboard. After that, she retired for the last time and married a Hong Kong millionaire.

Her tale is a classic *bildungsroman*: Portrait of the Artist As A Young Female Chinese Diver. But there is a curious twist. The means by which she expressed her hard-won freedom and autonomy were exactly the same as those that had been the expression of her subservience: diving, sport, victory. She defied the authorities by doing exactly what they wanted, but in a way that glorified the individual rather than the state; that glorified choice rather than coercion; that glorified sport rather than national prestige.

When I was in Beijing for the Olympic Games eight years later, I found the spirit of Fu much in evidence. I met some dazzling urbanites, spiritually enriched by foreign travel, a generation who can make the internet sing and dance its way round any silly old state prohibitions, who understand the modern world and how it works, and are anxious to relish its challenges and its rewards, its seriousness and its frivolities. I remember suggesting to one such, a very talented lady, that the young people of China were like young people living with their parents: tolerant enough so long as they are allowed to do exactly as they please; prepared to accept the situation so long as those in charge don't mess it up. That's it, she said, laughing at the analogy. I bought her another coffee on the strength of it.

Fu's story – the story of which she is the heroine – is a socio-political one, in the context of the emerging China, a country coming back into the world and discovering that you can't have the world on quite your own terms. If you enter the modern world, you will discover, belatedly, that your sons and your daughters are beyond your command. But Fu's tale is also an archetypal story, one of a young person coming of age and taking control of her world, controlling it as she controlled her flight through the air: lithe, graceful, courageous, her hair brushing the board.

47. David Beckham

DAVID BECKHAM'S STORY IS one of concealment: concealment followed by revelation. He is the fop revealed as hero: as if Osric, brutally treated by Hamlet for his affectations, decided not to referee the fencing but to take part and slay the prince himself. It is Sir Percy Blakeney dropping his pose as the ineffectual society drawler and revealing himself as the Scarlet Pimpernel. We English love a story of concealment, as we love to conceal ourselves behind social conventions: our national hero is, after all, Robin Hood, the outlaw hiding in the forest.

Like Tim Henman, Beckham came to prominence at Wimbledon in 1996; Henman by beating Yevgeny Kafelnikov, Beckham by beating the Wimbledon goalkeeper, Neil Sullivan, with a goal scored from a shot from within his own half. Beckham was instantly familiar: alarmingly young of face, and with a haircut, flopping over one eye, that was almost self-consciously feminine, even more so than George Best's. And he had extraordinary gifts as a footballer.

Beckham became a national hero, though he did so by the unusual route of becoming a national hate object first. He loved the role of hero, embraced it more fully than anyone. But ultimately, he was to fail: ultimately he was a hero of the Henman type, a hero who had the courage to try for everything, and therefore, the courage to fall short. There was a time when his penalty-taking for England became increasingly unreliable: his response was to keep taking them. When these failures cost him the job of penalty-taker, he said that, given the choice, he would have carried on, because he always believed he was going to score with the next one. There was something noble in that, in its daft way. That is his nature.

There is something noble about the entire Beckham story, even if Beckham's too-close association with daftness can never be removed from the story.

The tale of redemption is just one aspect of Beckham's tale, though it is the best one. In 1998, he was sent off when England played Argentina in the World Cup, in the round of 16. He was felled by the Argentinian captain, Diego Simeone. As Beckham lay face down on the ground, Simeone patronisingly – perhaps even brilliantly – ruffled his haircut. Beckham responded with petulant rage and gave Simeone a sharp little hack. Not enough to hurt Simeone: just enough to get himself sent off. England then fought a doomed rearguard action with immense spirit and almost won. Alas, they went out on penalties. And so it was Beckham's fault that England lost the World Cup, a story everybody was happy with, from the manager, Glenn Hoddle, through the press to the public. A pampered little poser was found out, and he cost England the world. He was hanged in effigy. He was already a celebrity who liked to be photographed with famous people and/or while wearing unusual clothes. His effigy, of course, wore a sarong.

The following domestic season began and Beckham was booed everywhere he went. Everyone said he would be better to move abroad, to leave the country that hated him with such passion, that the hatred would eventually destroy him. Beckham stayed. That was his nature. And the hatred had the exact opposite effect. That season, Manchester United, with Beckham playing a crucial role, won the unprecedented treble of Premier League, FA Cup and European Champions League. The two famous injury-time goals in the Champions League final both came from precisely struck Beckham corners.

Meanwhile, Hoddle was sacked as England coach for heresy, for saying that disabled people were paying the price for their sins in a former life. Kevin Keegan took over and then resigned in tears after defeat by Germany. So in came Sven-Goran Eriksson to try and save the day. His first move was to make Beckham captain. No one has ever loved a job title so much as Beckham loved being "England captain". And England started to move towards qualification. All England needed in the final match was a draw against Greece. But with 90 minutes gone, Greece were winning 2-1. Beckham had already tried and missed with a series of free kicks. Amazingly, in the few minutes added on, yet another free kick was awarded, more or less the last kick of the match, the last kick of the qualification campaign. And Beckham got that one right. With a sharp, devastating curl, it went into the goal as if there was no other place it could possibly go, and England were going to the World Cup after all. It wasn't great football: but Lord, it was great drama. Beckham could always supply that.

So the teasing gods that organise football put England against Argentina in the group stages: Argentina, one of the favourites for the tournament, still led by the haircut-ruffling Simeone. The tournament was in Japan and I was in Sapporo on that extraordinary night. The match turned on a penalty. Beckham took it himself. Confronted and insulted by Simeone, he lined up and blasted the ball down the middle. Pablo Cavallero in the Argentina goal didn't move. Had he reached out a hand, stuck out a leg, he could have stopped it. The ball almost brushed him, as Fu Mingxia's crew-cut used to brush the diving board. But he had subtly shifted his weight onto the wrong foot: it was as if he was stuck in concrete. And so the ball found the net and Beckham found redemption, and, it seemed, all the wrongs of history had been put right.

But with Beckham and England, things never reached the happily-ever-after stage that the narrative seemed to demand. England were knocked out in the quarter-finals by Brazil. Four years on, with the World Cup in Germany, England lost in the quarter-finals again, this time to Portugal.

The fact is that Beckham was never quite as good a footballer as he wanted to be. He dared to try and be the best player in the world: at his very best, he was in the top half-dozen. He wanted to lead England to glory in the World Cup: neither he nor his team were ever quite good enough.

There is, then, a tendency to blame him for the hopes he raised in us. Beckham has always divided opinions: though greatly loved, there have always been plenty of people to do the hating. One of the ostensible reasons for this is Beckham's love of celebrity: his famous wife, his famous friends, the celebrity events he attends, his advertisements for underpants. Beckham has never played the macho stereotype; unembarrassed about his own gentler nature. He loves to get dressed up, is delighted with his status as gay icon, is ostentatiously uxorious, and when he had a brief extra-marital fling, he shaved his hair and happily underwent a public pussy-whipping from his wife Victoria. He is an appropriately loving father. He hardly ever even has a drink.

This refusal to play the stereotype alienates some. Beckham always preferred a different kind of silliness to that of most famous footballers. There was courage in that, as well as originality. It takes a person deeply secure in himself to cut against the accepted norms of style and behaviour: Beckham found that security in his footballing talent. A man who can score 93rd-minute winners that take England to the World Cup: why, if he wants to wear a frock, then let him. Beckham was a triumphant footballer with a sexually ambiguous persona, and this novel combination caused many people to shift their notions of what gender is about and what real men can and can't do. Beckham was a hero with hints of the heroine about him: and that is at the heart of his achievement.

48. Ellen MacArthur

MAIDENS IN SUITS OF armour are always cropping up in romantic tales, so are princesses disguised as pageboys or squires, ambiguous heroine-heroes who sometimes accomplish mighty tasks traditionally associated with males. There was something of these archetypes in Ellen MacArthur, who took on the small task of conquering the world and actually did so. Twice.

These achievements made her greatly loved, mostly for the wrong reasons. She was also, in some circles, like David Beckham, rather resented, also for the wrong reasons. The fact was that her sexual ambiguity got people confused. She set off round the world on a boat the colour of a celluloid duck. It was called *Kingfisher*, and she sailed it by herself. She did all those tough-guy things with spanners and climbing the mast, and she also raced liked hell every yard of the way as she took part in the Vendee Globe single-handed round-the-world yacht race. She had very short hair, a crop apparently self-administered with nail scissors, and didn't trouble with any of the glamour stuff. A tough cookie, obviously. And yet when she had to get out of her boat at the end of the race, a race in which she finished second, she wept buckets, and kissed the boat as if it were a lover she was leaving on the quay. Later, when the documentary of her travels was released, there were some rather disturbing moments. MacArthur, out on the high seas, wept salt tears: "It's so hard," she would wail, again and again, in an ecstasy of self-pity. Some thought her the most terrible whinger: certainly, she didn't try and sell herself as an emotionally neutered hard man. My view is that anything that gets you round the Southern Ocean intact is the right thing. If you get round by weeping, then tears obviously have immense value.

The story had a great romance about it. MacArthur was triply vulnerable: alone, female and 5ft 2. The story was sexist and sizeist. McArthur saw her size, her sex and her emotional vulnerability as assets. It never occurred to her see to anything about herself as anything other than an asset.

She completed the Vendee in 2001. Four years later, she completed another solo circumnavigation, this time setting a new record of 71 days, 14 hours, 18 minutes and 22 seconds. I was there in Falmouth when she got back to Britain. This time she was not sailing cosy little yellow *Kingfisher*; she had a great brute of a trimaran, a racing monster, nakedly built for speed and entitled, with naked commercial intent, *B&Q*. I saw the impossibly tall mast appear off Pendennis Point, I saw the boat dock, I was there as the embracing of loved ones went on, and I was there when MacArthur spoke to the world afterwards. It was an astounding achievement: a brutally impressive piece of sport.

To understand this as pure sport, you must realise that this wasn't a tale of survival: the lone waif fighting the open oceans and the cruel sea. Not a bit of it. It is the story of a dedicated racer setting off in single-minded pursuit of a record. Every second was counted down by a clock on her boat. And while she was out on the ocean, she wasn't struggling to keep the boat afloat: she was trying to make it go as fast as it possibly could. She didn't undergo endless hours of sleep deprivation to keep death at bay: she was doing without sleep in order to get that extra half-knot of boat speed, to get the navigation right, to adjust to the wind shifts, to take account of all the information that was constantly being fed to her and to use it to gain more speed. She wasn't surviving, she was racing, she was competing, she was fighting, she was winning. She wasn't communing with nature: she was in hot pursuit of victory.

I spent some time with her a couple of years earlier, when she was about to set off on another record-seeking circumnavigation, this one with a crew. (It was a voyage that ended when the mast broke in the Southern Ocean.) I had a crash course in MacArthur: her singular nature, her deeply impressive and in some ways deeply disturbing personality.

"The waves were 30 feet. I was hand-steering for four hours at a time because the conditions were too much for the autopilot. And I loved it. You feel so lucky. Few people have ever seen this – when the waves break and the water goes white and there's a break and a little hint of blue. And then all at once a couple of dolphins came flying out of the waves – what the hell are you doing here? Haven't you seen the weather forecast?"

One of the problems with ocean racing is that the penalties for failure are rather more than a bollocking from the manager, or even being hanged in effigy. The penalty for failure is death; no doubt the rewards are correspondingly high. I wanted to talk to MacArthur about fear. We were in a café in Cherbourg; she was drinking something soft; I had a beer. But MacArthur had absolutely no interest in my topic of choice. In a bloke you'd write this off as macho posturing. With MacArthur I found something else, and it really rather worried me. It was as if she had something missing. "You want to be out there – so what's the problem?" She asked this as if she really wanted to know.

I couldn't let the question go. I have never been very happy on boats. Not my element. I had scrambled aboard *Kingfisher* at a press do a couple of year before, when MacArthur had sailed through Tower Bridge and I had ridden in a boat behind. MacArthur then tied up *Kingfisher* just downstream of the bridge, and I was permitted to scramble aboard and sit in the tiny cockpit, on the bench where she had curled up for her catnaps during her first great circumnavigation. I marvelled at the boat's cramped, stripped-down interior, MacArthur's universe for all those endless days, and then stepped ashore, feeling, I must confess, slightly sick. Not, as I said, my element. But it's MacArthur's. Never mind racing: "I'd sit on a barn door on a lake."

As we talked in the Cherbourg café, I hand-steered – conditions were too difficult to use autopilot – the conversation back to fear. "What are your options?" she asked. Well, one of them is not to start in the first place. That seemed not to have occurred to her. "Look, you have a problem, you find a solution. And the problem goes." As if it really was that simple. And perhaps for some people it really is.

MacArthur is utterly uncompromising. For such people, life has its simplicities. I was reminded of General Conyers, once again from a fragment in Anthony Powell: "His personality filled the room, though without active aggression. At the same time, he was a man who gave the impression, rightly or wrongly, that he would stop at nothing. If he decided to kill you, he would kill you; if he thought it sufficient to knock you down, he would knock you down; if a mere reprimand was all that was required, he would confine himself to a reprimand." MacArthur would similarly stop at nothing, and having killed you, if killing were necessary, would no doubt turn back to whatever it was that engrossed her: whatever else that needed to be done. It's no wonder she alienated some people – she wasn't quite like other people.

There was something of the spoiled saint in her, something of the same thing I found in Ayrton Senna, the devotion to the myth of oneself that brooks no refusal. But there was something sympathetic in her at the same time. She had about her a fine symbolic quality: we are, after all, all of us vulnerable people sailing the frail vessel of our lives across an uncompromising ocean, though not all of us are racing quite as hard as MacArthur. And I wondered: is she a person with a bit missing? Or with a bit extra? Does she lack the spirit of fear? Or does she possess the gift of faith?

"Have you ever doubted yourself?"

"Never."

Once more I nudged our course back towards fear: those 30-foot waves, the icebergs, the whales, the perfect storms. The question of fear. "I have never sat there and asked myself, why am I doing this? Never never never."

49. Usain Bolt

BY THE TIME YOU ARE in your fifth decade of watching sport, your notions of heroes and heroism have undergone profound changes. It would be highly to your discredit if they had not. It is not a simple journey from credulity to cynicism. It is far more interesting, far more complex than that. But if you are still watching sport, one thing at least is a constant: you still have your facility for amazement. As Steve Redgrave was unsated by victory, a person who loves sport is never sated by wonder. Like Cleopatra, like Katarina Witt, sporting wonder makes hungry where most it satisfies.

It was, not, then, with the wonder of a child that I watched Usain Bolt at the Olympic Games in Beijing in 2008. It was with the deeper wonder of a person who began watching sport by wondering at M.J.K. Smith and Anita Lonsbrough. Sport can still move me: it can still move anyone open to its wonders.

I watched every round of the 100 metres in Beijing, because I had a feeling that this might be an event that mattered. There were three athletes favoured for the gold medal, each with different credentials: Tyson Gay, Asafa Powell and Bolt. Bolt had set a world record of 9.72 but wasn't necessarily the favourite. He was very young, at 21. He hadn't much experience of the 100 metres; he had only seriously trained for the event that year. He hadn't the experience of the Olympic Games and of great expectation. No one knew how he would deal with these unique demands. Besides, he was an awkward starter: at 6ft 5, 1.96 m, he was a man who stood up in instalments. By the time he got going, the others might be off in the distance.

He more or less jogged through the first round. In the quarter-finals he ran 9.92 seconds slowing up; in the semis he made 9.85 look easy. He still looked as if he wasn't trying. By the time they lined up for the final, he was the clear favourite. I had a feeling that we were about to see something extraordinary. So, I suspect, did everybody else.

The tension before the 100 metres final at the Olympic Games is no manufactured thing. An athlete has one chance. Just one chance to get it right, one chance in four years. This is an event that lasts less than ten seconds. You must get it right between eyeblink and eyeblink. It is both a closed skill, yourself against the track, against the clock, and an open skill, a naked rivalry between eight supercharged men. Supercharged, one hopes, with natural forces. The memory of Ben Johnson lingers on.

Some deal with these pre-race tensions by blanking out the world, reducing all that's made to a tunnel 100 metres in length and one lane in width. Others go through stretches and warm-ups. Some ostentatiously flex muscles. Bolt just sort of loped up and grinned, his running vest hanging sloppily about his gangling frame. He got down onto his blocks, a long way down, and went into the sprinter's crouch. Ah, that fine, breathless hush: the ineffable silence of 90,000 voices, the tense anticipation before it all begins.

And, for the last time in this book, bang.

Bolt started well, but no better than the rest. The leaders were pretty much in line as they went through 40 metres. And then a miracle took place. Bolt just cruised away as if the rest had run into a patch of mud. For 40 or so metres he went into a different dimension of running: a different arena of human possibility. He put daylight between himself and the other runners, masses of daylight, built a lead that ought to have been impossible in so short a race, one featuring athletes of the same lofty standing in world sport. Bolt was winning by a distance. And then he danced.

It was as extraordinary a thing as I have ever seen in sport. With damn near 15 metres still to run, he abandoned running and performed the fastest boogie in history. He spread his arms wide, he slapped his chest twice, he lifted his knees ultra-high and went through the finish like Fred Astaire fired from a gun. Inevitably some criticised him for this, for he could have gone still faster. "I wasn't bragging," he said. "I was just happy." It was a glorious expression of immensely rapid joy. The finishing time was 9.69: a new second digit, the first time a six had ever followed the nine, the fastest run, the fastest man in history.

Bolt went on to win the 200 metres in another new world record, beating the Beamonesque time of Michael Johnson from the Atlanta Olympic Games of 1996. Bolt finished in 19.30, and then picked up a third gold with the Jamaica 4x100 metres relay. A year later, he went to the World Athletics Championships and did it all over again: a new digit on the 100 metres, finishing this time in 9.58, and beggaring belief as he followed this by winning the 200 metres in 19.19.

Not bad for a lad from Trelawny in Jamaica, not bad for the son of the local grocer, not bad for a boy who played football and cricket until he was persuaded by a schoolteacher to try a spot of track and field, not bad for a runner who was thought to be lazy and too much the joker. The joking seemed now to be an essential part of his ability: instead of the hyper-tense god-awful seriousness of the modern athlete who believes, that winning is the only thing, Bolt loafed towards the start grinning, making the odd quip, and treating it all as if it was the most tremendous lark. There was no feeling of life and death portentousness about it all: Bolt just ambled up and told humanity that it had under-estimated itself.

One of the great things that sport has done over the five decades I have been watching it is to make the most eloquent possible case for inclusiveness. It produced black heroes as well as white ones: and frequently black athletes have caused us to redefine the way we see the world and our own place in it. What Abebe Bikila told me over two and a bit hours, Bolt told me again 48 years later in not much more than nine seconds. Bolt wasn't barefoot, like Bikila in Rome: but he ran with one shoelace undone: the fastest shoelace the world has ever seen.

The possibility of greatness in a black person was no longer a revelation to me, as it was in 1960: it wasn't even a confirma-tion, because I hope I have gone beyond the point of needing such a thing confirmed. Rather it was the simple, unifying thing of joy. It wasn't a white boy's new understanding of the world: it was the purer joy of a human being's delight in the super-achievement of another, joy in the ultimate realisation of the human dream of speed. There was I, a white English-man brought up in Streatham, out there in China, a place where I had lived (though Hong Kong was then independent of the mainland government) for four happy and fulfilling years, watching a Jamaican whose ancestors were African and slaves to boot, showing us in a perfect symbolic form that humans are capable of achieving great things: fulfilling personal hopes, fulfilling the hopes of the world.

Not a highfalutin' conclusion at all: just an inevitable one: one told in 41 rather rapid strides.

50. Yelena Isinbayeva

BARON DE COUBERTIN, the man behind the modern Olympic Games, said that the function of women at his Games was to crown the victors with laurels. What, I wonder, would he have made of women's pole-vaulting? When I watched the film of the Woodstock music festival, the singer John Sebastian said from the stage: "Some cat's old lady's just had a baby!" What does he, or for that matter, what do I make of women's pole-vaulting?

I first watched women's pole-vaulting at the Olympic Games of 2000, in Sydney. I was supposed to be watching the men's triple jump at the time, but I found myself transfixed by the extraordinary beauty of the first women's pole-vault competition at the Olympic Games. Stacey Dragila, the American winner, was later to describe her event, not without irony, as "chicks on sticks". Here were women, for years thought too fragile to take part in so dangerous an event, casually leaping over the roof of my house. Here was a celebration of human athleticism, of female athleticism in particular; a celebration of courage and strength and technique and dedication.

I had never found all that much to be amazed at in the men's pole vault: splendid enough, yes, especially when performed by the matchless Sergei Bubka, but it never seemed to be anything particularly special. But when I saw women doing it, the contest enthralled from the first leap. Perhaps it was because, with the female physique, the combination of gymnastic ability with speed and power becomes far more vivid. Perhaps it is because, even when I watched the third Olympic competition, in Beijing in 2008, there was still a sense of the pioneer, the breaking of barriers, the destruction of taboo.

When Sebastian made his grotesque announcement at Woodstock, there was a part of me, young and imperfectly formed, that felt that here was a man in touch with the essential truths: that here was a man dressing the archetypal truths about men and women in the language of now; that the hippy movement was taking these fine traditions of the different roles of men and women, of cats and old ladies, and making them both modern and eternal.

I was to change my mind very swiftly. Almost at once, I was swept up in the hurricane of feminism: enraptured by the beauty of the notion that women's liberation, as the principle was first called, was nothing more nor less than human liberation, that by exalting women, men become more fully themselves. This is not a proposition I have subsequently dissented from.

Sport has been an important part of the breaking-down of barriers. In particular, sport has shown us that one race, one nationality, is not by definition superior to all others. This was the lesson of the Berlin Olympics of 1936, when Jesse Owens, a black American, beat the finest and blondest Aryans that the Nazis could dredge up. This was the lesson I learned in Streatham, when Abebe Bikila won the marathon in Rome. It was something we saw in the English domestic football of the 1970s, when managers would say: "I don't care if he's black or white or green with purple spots, if he can do a job for United he's in the team." Back then, that was progress, that was illumination, that was the stuff of revolution. Sport has made a considerable difference to race relations in Britain, the more so since black athletes came to represent Britain and

England and the Celtic nations in international competitions. England has had black footballers, rugby players, cricketers, track and field athletes and now a racing driver, and is the richer and the better as a result.

I would not claim that sport is invariably at the forefront of the breaking-down of barriers; it remains grossly lagged behind the world's pace in the acceptance of male homosexuality. But where sport led with the issue of race, it continues to work in the area of gender.

Yelena Isinbayeva was the daughter of a Russian plumber. She was talent-spotted and trained at a gymnast in Volgograd, but she rapidly grew too tall – she is now 5ft 8 ½ in, 1.74m. She was nudged towards track and field, and then to the pole vault. Here, she was able to combine the skill, daring and body-control of the gymnast with the power and speed required in the explosive events of the athletics stadium. Her technique is a thing of perfection, better than most, if not all men currently practising. This beauty, this effectiveness, is found most clearly in the L-phase: the point at which the athlete's body makes a feet-to-the-sky right angle, while the pole bends so that the top half is parallel with the ground, making an opposing, if curving, L. This is the phase that converts forward speed into upward flight. The rest, at the top of the flight, is all about minute, almost finicky control under duress.

I was there in the Bird's Nest Stadium in Beijing at the Olympic Games of 2008 to watch Isinbayeva win her gold medal. Not just win: to celebrate a triumph. The triumph of Isinbayeva, yes, of course, the triumph of the individual, but a lot more besides. This was also, it seemed to me, the ultimate symbolic expression of the triumph of womankind, the triumph of the feminism I learned when I was 20 and with it, the triumph of humanity.

Isinbayeva is one of the few athletes I have seen enter an athletics stadium with a duvet. She spent quite a lot of time lying under it as the rest of the field sorted itself out. Eventually, after getting on for two hours of competition between the lesser leapers, Isinbayeva emerged. She had delayed her entrance as a star, as a diva must: now taking the stage in carefully dramatic make-up and dolphin earrings. She has a special thing for dolphins. She then nonchalantly cleared the height at which she chose to begin. She didn't trouble to start competing seriously until most of the rest of her rivals had knocked down the bar enough times and had been eliminated. She then took her second jump at 4.85 metres, and that was enough to win the competition. But the event itself had hardly begun. With all the rest gone, Isinbayeva spent the next hour performing the Me Show: or the Women Show, or the Humanity Show. This was no longer the search for the winner, the search for the best: it had become a search for new possibilities. Isinbayeva had the bar set to 4.95, missed it twice but then cleared it to set a new Olympic record. After that she set the bar to 5.05. Failed twice. But the third time, she made it, leaping clear of the base earth as a breaching dolphin leaps clear of the sea. She fell from so great a height that she had time to celebrate on the way down. A new world record. Worth celebrating.

Oh, it was glorious to be there, glorious to see her, glorious to feel my heart soaring as this great athlete soared. Sporting heroes carry for each of us meanings far beyond those that the heroes themselves intend. Isinbayeva set out only to be a great athlete and, as a bonus, a great star: for me, her performance had a meaning that might even stretch as far as the salvation of the human race. That is sport for you: it not only beguiles: it stands for things. That is the nature of sport's heroes: they not only perform extraordinary things, they also, whether they like it or not, come to stand for some of the great and important matters of life.

This is a personal thing for each spectator, for each person who amasses an individual collection of heroes through a lifetime of watching sport. M.J.K. Smith didn't intend to make me aware of the fragility of human hopes and the perpetual proximity of personal limitation; Olga Korbut didn't intend to make me aware that brilliance and ambition and courage can be found far from the domain of machismo; Ian Botham didn't intend to make me believe that extraordinary things can take place against common sense and logic; Steffi Graf didn't intend to make me understand the power of self-determination, of personal conquest of a troubled past; Steve Redgrave didn't intend to make me feel that relentless ambition can threaten the dominion of time. But they all did – and those are just the members of this panheroikon whose chapter numbers end with a one.

Isinbayeva means more than she could possibly have intended, as all sporting heroes must. The world is in crisis, and for a reason seldom admitted: because of over-population. The most important potential answer to over-population is to be found in the education and the exaltation of women. If the human race has a long-term prospect, it is to be found in the ascent of woman. At the Olympic Games of 2008, Isinbayeva became – at least for me – that symbol of exaltation, that symbol of hope.

The job of a hero in sport – the reason our minds, rooted in archetypes, create for each of us a personal collection of heroes, our own individual panheroikon – is to make sense of life, to make some kind of order from a crazy and chaotic world. This is a process that tends to bypass such humdrum matters as logic and sense and even self-respect. Our heroes educate us throughout our lives. They cast piercing beams of illumination onto the world we live in, and, since most heroes tend to be the victorious ones, fill us with at least some kind of hope, however deluded. With Isinbayeva's soaring clearance of my roof, I knew perfectly well that the problems of life had not been solved, but that hope still existed: that the hopes of humanity could be symbolised, if not realised, in the cheetah-fast boogie of Usain Bolt and in the dolphin-flight of Isinbayeva.

Classification

By species:

 Human *Homo sapiens*   47
 Horse *Equus caballus*   3

By gender

 Male   39 ½ *
 Female   9 ½ *
 Gelding   1

By sport

 Cricket   12
 Track and field   8
 Tennis   7
 Football   6
 Racing   3
 Aquatics   2
 Equestrianism   2
 Rugby   2
 Skating   2
 American football   1
 Boxing   1
 Gymnastics   1
 Motor racing   1
 Rowing   1
 Yachting   1

* Torvill and Dean

By Nationality*

Great Britain and Northern Ireland   20
USA   7
Barbados   2
Australia   1
Brazil   1
Canada   1
China   1
Czechoslovakia   1
East Germany   1
Ethiopia   1
Fiji   1
France   1
Germany   1
Holland   1
Ireland   1
Jamaica   1
Italy   1
New Zealand   1
Poland   1
Russia   1
Sri Lanka   1
Sweden   1
Switzerland   1
USSR   1

* Some of these countries no longer exist. Some of the heroes changed nationality. In all cases I have used the nation each hero first represented.

In case of difficulty in purchasing any Short Books
title through normal channels, please contact
BOOKPOST Tel: 01624 836000
Fax: 01624 837033
email: bookshop@enterprise.net
www.bookpost.co.uk
Please quote ref. 'Short Books'